Dear Carmen

You are a pearl of great ...
and the World is Your Oyster.
So good to meet you.
Enjoy!
Love
Marcia

Published by Success Maker Marcia M.
©Copyright Marcia M 2016

All rights reserved.
This book is sold subject to the condition that it is not, by way of Trade or otherwise, be lent, hired out or otherwise circulated in Any form of binding or cover other than that in which it is published. No part of this publication may be reproduced, stored in a retrieval system, or transmitted in any form or by any means (electronic, mechanical, photocopying, recording or otherwise) without prior written permission from Success Maker Marcia M.

ISBN-13:
978-1530606566

ISBN-10:
153060656X

Printed by Create Space an Amazon Company

This is a work of fiction, based on a true life story, names, characters, places, Dialogues and incidents are used fictitiously.

www.marciamspence.com

Geraldine's Pearl A Spirit of Power, Love and a Sound Mind

Geraldine's Pearl by Marcia M

Geraldine's Pearl by Marcia M

Illustration of Grandma Geraldine by Fiona Faye

Geraldine's Pearl by Marcia M

Geraldine's Pearl
A Spirit of Power, Love and a Sound Mind
Marcia M.

Endorsement

"Anyone who reads Marcia's book will gain a deep appreciation of the spirit within all of us that has the power to keep bouncing us back up again after every fall. This is more than just a story of survival against all odds, but it is a story that gives hope that in spite of horrible circumstances we can thrive!"

Dicken Bettinger, Ed.D., licensed psychologist retired, founder of 3 Principles Mentoring and author of Coming Home: Uncovering the Foundations of Psychological Well-being.

Geraldine's Pearl by Marcia M

Commendation

This book is a powerful lesson in being courageous "it takes courage to interrogate yourself, it takes courage to look in the mirror and see past your reflection to who you really are when you take off the mask" (C West). Marcia is a living epistle defining a redemptive story that lays bare the catastrophic that wrestles with the greatness planted in us by God. The clue is wrapped deeply in the title Pearls are made in a dark place of pressure layer after layer of a substance called nacre (calcium carbonate) forming a perfect pearl of great value. This book takes you on the journey that has made a pearl of great price to find it you must fight fear and embrace a new love ethic given by God.
God hath not given us the spirit of fear; but power, and of love, and of a sound mind (2 Timothy 1:7 The Bible)

I commend this book to you as not just a story but a new personal revelation of your own courageous step to finding the greatness that God has put inside of you.

Revd Dr Jonathan Jackson
Senior Pastor NTCG The Rock
Bishop of NTCG Highgate District of Churches

Geraldine's Pearl by Marcia M

Special Reviews

My daughter Marcia.M is an intelligent, strong, hardworking woman, she has an amazing ability to bounce back, she is not a woman to be kept down, and she is always pushing herself and has a thirst for knowledge. Marcia is a passionate woman who puts her heart and soul in whatever she does. Writing this book has been emotional as she maps out her life journey. I as her mother found the book difficult to read with tears in my eyes. However it is done and I am so very proud of her bravery. Well done my daughter love you always – **Mom.**

Marcia 'The Success Maker' is the name that I gave my mother to name her business about 4 years ago as that is all that I see my mother as, a success! Her unconditional love for me and my siblings is the epitome of what I believe is a perfect mother in my eyes, whether it be tough or the softest, sweetest love that you could experience. My mother is my biggest critic but also my greatest support, she is a true ambassador for women, always sees good in everyone and strives to help people become their best: often putting others before herself.

This book 'Geraldine's Pearl' has made me even more proud of my mother, I didn't know that my pride in her could reach another height. I am amazed at the strength she has after enduring so many obstacles. I believe that this story connects with women and men of all ages and stages of life and is a story of a child, young lady, a woman, a mother, daughter, wife, a human!!! A real woman of power and influence! Congratulations mom. I love you so much - **Your eldest daughter.**

Geraldine's Pearl
A Spirit of Power, Love and a Sound Mind
Marcia M.

Dedications:

This book is dedicated to the memory of my grandmother, Geraldine; I will forever be 'Geraldine's Pearl'. I know that you are resting in peace. I hope that I continue to make you proud.

To My Mother who is my wonder woman, whose bravery and love has no bounds.

To my father and stepfather, thank you for the important roles that you have played in my life, I love you both.

To My children; my Son, my Daughters and Grandsons, who are my reasons for being.

My dear Son - thank for allowing me the freedom to tell our story despite you being a very private person.

To my baby girl, I thank you so much for the day to day sacrifices that you have made and the maturity and understanding that you have shown during the writing and production of this book.

My beloved eldest daughter, thank you for providing constructive feedback on early versions of this book; I know it's been hard for you coping without my company for many months.

To the men whom I have loved - thank you for allowing me to share our story.

Geraldine's Pearl by Marcia M

I have deep gratitude to my siblings (and brothers and sister in law) who all believed in me and motivated me to tell my story, which is also part of their story.

Many Thanks to Sophie and Dawn Spence who empowered and encouraged me to stand in my truth.

I also wish to thank my Editor, Maureen Elizabeth Worrell, [multiple award winning Author], for her loving, tender, sisterly support and kindness in enabling me to complete my book, despite her own ill health, which took a serious turn during the editing process. I have not the words to express my gratitude and love to and for you.

DJ Countryman, I thank you for believing in me and for being a tower of strength as I completed this book.

Annika Spalding and Jenice Revers fellow authors, my role models and advisors I thank you both for your advice and guidance.

Cynthia Gaynor for my cover Photography & Victoria Breakwell, who worked patiently on this awesome book cover design.

Many thanks and love goes out to Bishop Jonathan Jackson, Janet Rhynie, Steve Kaye & Dicken Bettinger, for being facilitators to my journey.

And finally, to all of the **'Success Makers and Woman of Power & Influence Community'** as well as listeners of **'On the Couch'**, thank you for being the tribe who I love to serve.

Marcia M

FOREWORD:

Maureen Elizabeth Worrell

'Geraldine's Pearl: A Spirit of Power, Love and Sound Mind' – is a fabulously written book charting the devastating, truthful and long-lasting impact that growing up and living with domestic violence and domestic abuse has on a child, who then has to navigate her way through life and into adulthood, bearing the scars of not having had the luxury of resources to have dealt with how domestic violence and sexual abuse affected every aspect of her life.

As the main character narrates her story we are given a powerful insight into how affected she is by having to struggle on a daily basis, to find her place and identity, not only in the world, but amongst her immediate and extended family and those she interacts with at school and in the work place.

'Geraldine's Pearl' – "You are a Pearl of Great Price" - her grandmother very often reassured her. The sad irony is that this little girl did not fully understand the profound meaning of those words, spoken with a deep and unconditional love to her, until she was well into her mid-forties.

Geraldine's Pearl by Marcia M

The very connotations of this beautiful phrase has the reader wanting to immediately know more about her life experiences and her survival, which is inclusive of failed relationships and marriages, divorce, emotional and mental abuse, chaos and trauma, as she battles to save her beloved children from choosing a misguided path as they grow amidst the tense and often times chaotic dramas of what proves to be their life experiences that destiny has placed before them.

This is a book that epitomises the internal strength and faith of several women through the generations and of how, with her feisty and determined belief that she will obtain her dreams of having a peaceful and loving family life and home, the main character battles through and overcomes a minefield of various crisis that could easily have defeated a person of lesser character or strength to overcome and rise above the multitude of negativities and crisis that shaped her life for so many years.

You will find it intriguing to read how it would have been far easier to succumb to the anguish, betrayals and misunderstandings that befall the author of this really good and empowered read. It is a story of love, romance, abuse, isolation, struggles, heartache, faith, survival and success.

Geraldine's Pearl by Marcia M

It is an honest account of feelings and thoughts and of owning those emotions towards finding a way to battle through and emerge stronger than before.

The author, Marcia M, is an inspiring Business Woman, Coach, Speaker, Mentor, Talk Show Host and Writer, who has worked diligently and tirelessly to carve out a successful career for herself despite all she had to endure. The bouts of depression and debilitating illnesses could not stop her from standing firm in attempting to rise above and to become all that she believed she could be.

As a survivor of childhood sexual abuse and childhood domestic violence and abuse myself, and the honoured and humbled recipient of six [6] various Awards for my own book, 'The Journey of I & I' - I was immediately drawn into her story from the very first page. Once you read her story, you are left feeling empowered and more hopeful. With each page that I read, I was reminded of my life's mantra of: 'Set Peace of Mind as Your Goal and Work Towards Achieving That Goal on a Daily Basis' – just as the author's life mantra is: 'The Greatest Revenge is Success' – something that as a reader of her book, you are intrigued and eager to read on to see if she does indeed achieve this in part, if not in all, of her life, as she endeavours to pick herself up from one disaster after another to hold her head up high with joy, peace and love for herself and others, inclusive of those who have caused her hurt and harm.

I have personally known this author for some years but even so, her written words surpassed all of my eagerly anticipated expectations, especially as this is her first published book. Her personal and business brand of being epitomised as 'The-Bounce-Back-Ability-Queen' is well justified and apt. Read her story and this particular meaning will become apparent.

This is a book that is highly recommended for all to read and to gain some form of the gift of feeling uplifted and re-empowered, as you begin to understand the complexities of growing up within an environment of domestic violence and abuse of all types. 'Geraldine's Pearl' not only honours the author's story but will also honour and validate mine and your stories also.

Maureen Elizabeth Worrell

Multiple Award Winning Author of 'The Journey of I & I' and the soon to be published 'The Definition of I & I'

REEBA Outstanding Achievement Award. Back2Back BAFTA Inspirational Award. BEFFTA Best Author Award. Lift Effects Inspirational Star Award. Lift Effects Inspirational Star of All Stars Runner Up Award.

REEBA Best Counsellor of the Year Award. Leadership Mind Ambassadors [LMA] International Best Female Creative Author of the Year Award. Nominated for a Lift Effects Star/Star of All Stars Inspirational Award.

Qualified Counsellor in Childhood Sexual Abuse & Domestic Violence & Abuse. Inspirational Speaker. Mentor. Qualified Book Manuscript Editor. Ambassador to Free Your Mind Mental Health. Ambassador to Skye Alexandra House for Vulnerable Young Ladies. Administrator & Activist for 'WE HAVE LOVED ONES MISSING TOO' [highlighting the missing profile cases of missing black children and adults].

Geraldine's Pearl
A Spirit of Power, Love and a Sound Mind.

Marcia M.

Prologue:

I wrote sections of this book over a period of ten years, initially because writing down my pain and frustrations helped me to release those hidden emotions and saved me from hurting someone else with my actions based upon anger and other negative feelings of hurt. I also used my jottings as a means to reflect on how far I have emotionally travelled and healed from anguish, that at the time seemed never ending.

At the point of putting together this prologue, I am a forty-eight year- old woman with three children aged twenty-nine, twenty-six and fourteen years old. I also have two grandsons, one who is almost five years of age and another who is just under 18 months old. I have a son in-law and daughter in-law who I also love like my own children.

Geraldine's Pearl by Marcia M

I am truly blessed in that I have five siblings, all of whom I love deeply. My beloved parents have lived abroad for almost ten years and my biological father lives in the local area. I come from two huge extended families all of whom too, I love very dearly.

My children were fathered by two men: the two loves of my life. I loved these men individually, each with a different type of love and they both gave me experiences of love on different levels but most importantly, they gave me my offspring, my children, my family and for that reason, I will always have love for them both.

It is now 2016. At this point in our lives, the significant men in my children's and my life are both at two ends of an awful, insidious, home wrecking spectrum: one of them is incarcerated on suspicion of supplying Class A drugs and the other is addicted to alcohol & crack cocaine.

The impact of their life choices have left all of my children feeling bereft, confused and disappointed. I struggle at times as I feel that it was my own poor choices that have brought this pain to my children and to me. However, I write this book from a place of complete self-love, self-care, understanding and compassion for me.

I share my experiences of life and its tumultuous hills and valleys that have taught me how to find the deepest level of love, peace and joy. It is from that place that I am able to have compassion for others and can give and share love with many people. I have been broken down so many times that I no longer feel any shame about the circumstances that I find myself in as I know that my peace, joy and love is, going forwards, unshakeable.

To everyone and/or anyone who may be mentioned or alluded to in this book, I thank you for sharing your lives with me in the journey called life: my intention here is to uplift the power of healing, the power of love, of self-love, care and understanding. This book recognises the human-ness, imperfection and fallibility of us all.

Geraldine's Pearl by Marcia M

To anyone who feels that they may have hurt me, I forgive you totally and I thank you for the experience, as I know that I have hurt others too along my personal journey, some in ways that I do not even know or realise the gravity of the pain I may have caused someone else.

This book is here to share, to assist the reader in finding ways to overcome; this book is an act of love to myself and is about my truth, my life and my perspective.

I am joyful at being content and in a place where despite accepting no paid work for over six months so that I could focus on writing and with bills building up around me, I am filled with a peace and joy that is totally beyond my own understanding. I am also enjoying life and having fun as I am beginning to understand that my life is not my own and I'm cruising and enjoying the emotional, mental and visible scenery that is both in and around me.

As you take the time to read my story, please find love and compassion for every character as you try to put yourself in my shoes and in so doing, you will then also empathise with,

Geraldine's Pearl by Marcia M

understand and forgive the other people involved, for this is exactly what I had to do to bring about my own internal healing.

I feel love.
I share love.
I am love.

Geraldine's Pearl

Geraldine's Pearl by Marcia M

Starting Point

My parents married at the ages of twenty and twenty-one years of age, my father being the elder of the two. I was their first child born in January 1968. They had married just three months before my birth in October 1967 and my first home was in my paternal grandparent's large Victorian house located in the inner city of Lozells, Birmingham, an area that during my childhood we called 'Bottom Handsworth'. These larger properties had attracted the migrants from the Caribbean and Asia in the late 50's and early 60's where more than one family shared the cost of purchasing and running the house.

My grandparents' home was huge with six bedrooms, three large double bedrooms on the first floor and one of the downstairs rooms converted to a bedroom plus two rooms in the attic. There was also a basement/cellar, although I do not recall ever venturing down there to see the layout.

Geraldine's Pearl by Marcia M

My newly married parents lived in one of the first floor bedrooms. Jamaican by birth, they had met two years previously and swiftly married before I was born, as was the custom in the 1960's. Single and unmarried parenting was frowned upon in those days for it was seen as bringing shame on the family, so my parents did what was considered the right thing to do and married in a church, embracing the traditional white wedding which was duly organised by my maternal grandmother.

My first year of life was spent living at my paternal grandparents' home in 'Gordon Road' in the house where my father's brothers and their wives and girlfriends and fiancés also lived or conducted their courtships. My younger uncle and aunt were young children themselves when I was born.

My father Neville had five brothers and one sister and my father was the second eldest child of the marriage with his older brother being the one surviving twin.

Geraldine's Pearl by Marcia M

It was reiterated to me that I was a very beautiful baby with beautiful eyes - "Eyes that would break many hearts"; my mother's brother had told her as he held me in the hospital after my birth. I was a special baby, bestowing the titles of 'Aunt' and 'Uncle' upon my mothers' siblings for the first time. Those eyes are now forty-eight years old and may have broken some hearts but they surely have also shed many, many tears

Geraldine's Pearl by Marcia M

Chapter One

Early Years

At the time of my birth, my mother was a Nurse and my father was employed as a Jewellery Engraver. My father, tall, at least 6ft I believe, was a slim, very handsome young man with soft, black, neatly groomed hair, quiet, very attractive, not chatty but quiet in a kind of thoughtful way.

Mom (the first daughter born to my maternal grandmother), was a very pretty, petite, vivacious, freckle-faced, light skinned, Jamaican woman, intelligent and ambitious. My mother, as with many Jamaican children, was raised by her doting maternal grandparents in the Westmoreland countryside; she grew up alongside her cousin and younger aunt. My great grandfather's skin tone was completely white and he had blond hair and my great grandmother was of another racial mix with their children having white skin and long hair and the boys being slightly more brown in their

Geraldine's Pearl by Marcia M

complexion. This was the legacy we inherited from slavery. We are typical Jamaicans, 'Out of Many One People', and my father's family was of a similar mix as is so common across the island and parishes of Jamaica.

My mom has recounted many stories of her childhood of how she and her cousin got up to naughty antics and the 'beatings' (hidings) her cousin would get when they got caught, although my mom reckons that she could run so fast that they couldn't catch her to physically chastise her. My mother was known to her family by her 'pet' name/family name, 'Olive', as it is rare for a Jamaican person of that time and even my generation to be known or addressed by their registered legal name. There are many Jamaicans who are not registered as born on the true day of their birth, some by a difference of a day or a week or, as in my mother's case by a month. I have heard tales of people who do not even know their year of birth, particularly those from poor rural communities, who struggled to physically or financially make the trip to the city in time to register their child's true birthdate. Being registered a month later than her birth wasn't viewed negatively by my mom

Geraldine's Pearl by Marcia M

because she embraced it; it was just a simple fact of her life. We always celebrate mom's birthday in August on her actual true birthdate, you see our mom is a proud Leo lioness, she also relished the fact that she had two birthdays and likened herself to the Queen, the only downside is that she has had to wait an extra thirty days to officially reach milestones such as pension age, bus pass etc.

My father, on the other hand, attached shame to the week difference in his birthdate and insists on dismissing the true date, only to recognise the official registration date. This is just one small example of the different outlooks on life that my parents have: my father would see the negatives and mom the positives, always, no matter what the circumstances.

Eleven months after my birth my younger brother Adam was born, then twelve months after his birth another brother Peter was born; our young mother at only twenty-two years of age, had given birth to three children within the space of two years which consequently took its toll on her health and on the health of her child who sadly didn't survive more than

Geraldine's Pearl by Marcia M

a few days. After another two years' break, my sister Amanda was born.

We lived in our own house by then on Newcombe Road, a terraced two-bedroom house in the part of Handsworth, Birmingham, we called 'Top Handsworth'. My parents were the first of their siblings to buy their own home and it was a real accomplishment at their young ages. Our home was nicely furnished and very clean. We were fed well as mom was an excellent cook and mother, and we had good routines for bed time, bath time, and weekly hair washing in the bath. I HATED hair washing day! I have a memory of one of the days when I was about five years of age being told "Lie back Marcia" so that mom could pour the water over my head and me not wanting to lie back in the bath because I was afraid of the water splashing over my face and getting in my eyes and ears. I didn't like the feeling of it as it had scared me. I had fought my way out of my mother's grip, screaming hysterically and swiftly jumped out of the bath and whilst running out of the front door, somehow, I had slipped my red velveteen

Geraldine's Pearl by Marcia M

nighty on, I don't know how and I'm unsure of what I had on my feet but I was running away most determinedly.

Determination - that is definitely one of my characteristics, focussed a head full of ideas, thoughts and philosophies, plans and visions. As a young girl I loved to sing, dance and perform. I wrote plays and directed shows with my brother and sisters and sometimes with my cousins, willingly and maybe unwillingly, but at the time I wouldn't have noticed their reluctance in taking part and playing their roles in the band, musical or play. I loved drama. I also loved to read and I would read books, fiction and non-fiction, every night in bed before I slept. I read during the day time too. I had an insatiable thirst for knowledge, I was curious about the world, about life, about facts.

I would get lost in my storybooks, 'Ann of Green Gables,' 'The Secret Diary of Adrian Mole', 'The Family Medical Encyclopaedia' and comics and magazines such as 'Whizzer and Chips' and 'Jackie'. Our mom was excellent at supplying reading materials and taking us to the library and she often

Geraldine's Pearl by Marcia M

bought book sets for us. Mom was the type of mother who was engaged in her children's learning and did her best in providing writing and creative materials that we needed to study at home. Mom also sat on every school governing body for all of our schools, which in itself was amazing!

I vaguely remember going to Saturday School and on trips and visits to museums and many places of interest across the UK and locally in and around Birmingham. Mom was and still is a focussed mother who loves her brood dearly, she is a woman of immense class, built with tenacity and determination, and she is an achiever and one of the finest examples of 'Mother Love'. She has demonstrated with her life how to overcome adversity, to follow your dreams and to achieve your aspirations. Becoming an adult I grew to admire every aspect of my mother's being, her beauty, her personality, her feisty, fiery 'lioness-ness,' she is a true Leo, formidable and yet possesses a compassionate and loving spirit.

This compassion is no better illustrated than when in the late 60's, living within her in-law's home, she cared for her new

Geraldine's Pearl by Marcia M

baby girl alongside a baby boy who belonged to one of the daughters of the family who lived next door. Such kindness she extended to the younger woman than she afforded even to herself, to enable this young mother to go out to work. The depth of this kindness I shall now reveal. The baby boy was six months older than her own baby, a beautiful baby boy, with lovely brown skin a slightly darker tone than her own child. My mother gave the baby tender loving care as is the right of any child. The child had a closer connection to her in that he was in fact my father's first child by a girl who lived with her parents next door to my grandparents. How amazing, what strength of character, that despite her partner fathering this child whilst in a relationship with her, she was able to care for the child - that is the depth of love and strength of my mother.

The facts of the matter are that my brother was born six months prior to my birth and three months before my parents' marriage. A year later, my brother's mother married and her husband adopted my brother and raised him as his own son. Later I will tell you more about my brother and of

Geraldine's Pearl by Marcia M

how we were reunited about forty-five years after these events.

Chapter Two

Childhood

So, as far as my childhood is concerned, I have said in the past that I do not really remember being happy, yet as I now continue to write, I have an internal feeling of joy for there are moments etched in my memory of playing with my siblings and cousins, running wild and free during the long hot summer holidays. I also loved school, I was bright, gifted and talented in many areas and I was eager to learn. I also wanted to be 'good' even though by nature I was mischievous, so I tried my best not to get into trouble as I didn't like getting told off. I always wanted to receive approval and to be approved of.

I was a naturally curious child, inquisitive, vocal, a child of action and challenge, and I often did and said things that other children wouldn't, and I'm a bit like this even now! I suppose I was what some adults may have called cheeky and defiant. Despite being a girl I was very boisterous, I loved to climb, jump and explore, I was physically strong and very

Geraldine's Pearl by Marcia M

agile, mentally alert and a skilled talker and negotiator, I was a bossy child; I was always in charge.

My cousin once shared with me when we were in our thirties, that when we were children he loved being with me because I was the only child who would stand up to the adults: apparently I always did and my younger family members appreciated it. I don't remember doing this but I do recall having a strong sense of injustice as I had my own perspective on life and had developed a real belief in justice and equality for all, especially children.

My childhood consisted of multiple levels of existence: fantasy, play, fun, freedom, using my imagination to see myself in the characters that I was reading about. I read stories of young girls, heroes and heroines, happy ending stories that gave me hope for the future, alongside the realities of early sexualisation and living through the trauma of domestic violence.

Geraldine's Pearl by Marcia M

At a very young age I had experienced a teenagers' hot penis being placed in my mouth. To this day I remember it vividly. He had told me that it was his finger but for many years that memory haunted me, the horrid realisation that this warm 'thing' that I had tasted that had been inserted into my mouth, the mouth of a five year - old little girl: how disgusting, what an abuse and an audacity that a relative should see fit that he could remove my underwear whilst telling me gently to "Close your eyes", and of course I obeyed as any little child would. I trusted him even when he had then said "Open your mouth". It's sickening to me as I write it, how awful! And as he placed his thing into my open trusting mouth which I closed around 'it' he said, "It's my finger." I didn't know what it was and I didn't open my eyes. Horrifying!

This was rape, I know this now but at five years of age how was I to comprehend what was had been done to me? How? So for my protection I believe my mind pushed the experience into my subconscious for preservation of my mind and self. It took until my teens when I became sexually active, for the

Geraldine's Pearl by Marcia M

memory to return and for me to put the pieces of the crime that had been committed against me together.

These are not memories that I cherish, I would prefer not to remember, but they do underpin the woman that I am today and have impacted on my adult sexual experiences.

Growing up, there was the adult world and the children's world, with the children sometimes playing games of pretending to be adults that were highly inappropriate and sexualised and in hindsight it was not nice but it seemed at the time that it was a just a fact of our life.

In those days, children didn't seem to have many rights except perhaps the fragile freedom to play, as long as we didn't make too much noise or break anything. Whenever we were at my maternal grandmother's home we ate at a small table and often, because there were so many of us, we ate at various sittings and we drank water with our meals and sometimes squash. Grandma was a good cook and her stew chicken and curry goat and rice and peas were to die for, the gravy and rice alone was enough to tantalise and satisfy your taste buds.

My maternal grandmother was a business woman, a dressmaker and designer of wedding gowns, in fact she made all clothing, and she even made lingerie for us all. Often I, my younger sisters and my aunts, would own an item of clothing made to measure for each of us, cut from the same cloth. My sister and I were always coordinated and dressed in identical clothes.

Grandma also made wedding cakes to order as she ran a thriving business working from home so there was never the need for her to go out to work. This also meant that as grandma was consistently home, her children were guaranteed a babysitter when they needed one and therefore my early childcare was spent in the company of my dear grandmother's care and attention. Grandma was the epitome of a matriarch and as the head of her household she ensured that we were fed, clean and well-groomed and dressed always.

Geraldine's Pearl by Marcia M

Grandad was a gentle spirit, an attractive, dapper man, with a mischievous look; he worked in a Foundry for most of his years here in the UK. Grandad brought his wages home every week and grandma would manage the budget, displaying how she was very thrifty and extremely astute in saving and financial planning. Grandma was always involved in a 'partner' and sometimes ran a partner for the family. Partner, pronounced *'Paardna!'* was a weekly or monthly savings/loan club where each member paid their instalment or made their deposit, this was called *'throwing your hand'* and for example if seven people joined and paid £50 each month, every member in turn would receive a payment of £600, the 'hands' that each of the other members had 'thrown' and this was called collecting your 'Paardna draw'. These schemes helped people to purchase large items of furniture or particularly to pay for flights back home and in the early days in the UK, to pay deposits for homes.

Grandma encouraged her whole family to save, she also gave me tips on how to hide money around the house; her favourite hiding place was under the carpet in the toilet.

Geraldine's Pearl by Marcia M

My maternal grandmother's home was bright and busy and well organised by the matriarch that was affectionately known as 'Gong Gong'. In contrast, at my paternal grandparents, the atmosphere was different, it was very masculine and Grandad was the ruler over his family, his wife, his six sons and his daughter. William also attempted to control his daughters-in-law.

The house was clean and well organised and my father's parents' home was large, with high quality furnishings but the atmosphere was often tense and as a direct result, my paternal grandma was quiet and flat and appeared cold like a stranger, kind of indifferent, and grandad was loud and booming with a deep powerful voice. He was very tall, over six feet and as a child I was aware of his huge feet, well actually huge shoes, which would be hanging on the shoe rack in my grandparents' bedroom. My grandfather must have been about fifty years of age, well established financially and young enough to enjoy his life. The air was filled with the sounds of men, my uncles, grandad and extended family; they had a colour television in the front room on which they would watch

Geraldine's Pearl by Marcia M

'rastleing' (wrestling), horse racing and cowboy movies. I was born into this house as the first grand-daughter and like many of my cousins, this was my first home as my grandparents provided accommodation to their sons and their new wives, so in the late 60's and early 70's, the family expanded.

At home with mom and dad at Newcombe Road, a typical two- bedroom terraced house, next door to the corner shop, lived the husband, wife and two children, a boy and girl, me and my younger brother, Adam. The house was a typical 70's home with bright patterns of oranges and yellows and faux leather sofas and a coffee table in the front room. I shared a bedroom with my brother and most nights we slept well but then other nights we were awakened by the sounds of banging and crashing and cries and shouts, an indication of my father and mother fighting. I do not know how my mother coped with being abused and violated as she was. They were both still so young, in their early twenties.

Chapter Three

Neville!

Let me try and describe my father. How can I describe my father? I often try to describe him as a man who has some mental health issues and has for most of his life since his teens. I believe that this is something that he recognises now and has found his own kind of peace with this in his later life and at this moment of writing, he is approaching seventy years of age.

I love my father dearly and always wish the best for him; I also appreciate that he loves me too as he has never given up on trying to maintain a relationship with me and my children and I believe he will never stop and that is to his credit. As a child, then a teen and ultimately into my adulthood, I was a dutiful daughter, of all of my siblings I visited him the most quite regularly and maintained a relationship with him after my parents' separation. I needed him, I loved him, he was my dad.

Geraldine's Pearl by Marcia M

I would make efforts to call him and catch buses to see him or invite him to my home for meals and gatherings. I have organised birthday celebrations for and with him and we decorated my new home together. I do not want you to get the wrong impression as we have had a relationship my whole life.

I will now however attempt to describe the impact his behaviour has had on my life.

For me it is a horror story, an emotional horror story, not a story filled with joyful experiences and memories. My dad is the type of person who lives in his own head most of the time and does not really engage in anything that is happening beyond his own thoughts. A person whose behaviour by word and deed I have found abhorrent, yes that's how I would describe it - 'abhorrent'.

My words to describe his presence would have to be: offensive, eccentric, non-caring, ridiculing, misogynistic, paranoid, bullying, moody and narcissistic. My father, for his

Geraldine's Pearl by Marcia M

children, is the one person that you do not really want to speak to on the telephone, and who terrifies us at the thought of him knocking our front doors.

I do not believe that my father really knows me at all, he has never spent the time to sit and listen and relate to me and unfortunately for most of my life, I have lived in fear of the contents of his mind over-spilling and the way that manifests in physical violence or verbal abuse. These manifestations and the fear of them have brought me significant angst throughout my whole life. I often wished that he would just listen, engage, and show some real care and understanding. I wished that he was someone that I could turn to if ever I was in need. It has occurred to me that maybe I could, but I have either never tried or maybe I have asked but learnt never to ask again.

I do recall how in the last five years, just before I started public speaking, having called him to share how the experiences of my childhood had affected me and the disappointment I felt that he wouldn't listen. He told me that

Geraldine's Pearl by Marcia M

he had paid the price for his conduct by losing his wife and children and that he did not want to talk about it. This was hard for me to take as I felt that we needed to talk about it, I wanted him to know my pain and I wanted his help, his comfort and his understanding. I was seeking an avenue for there to be closure so that we could move forward but my father didn't need that as he had moved on from it. *It is understandable that he may not have the ability to comprehend and fully appreciate the lifelong, lasting effects possible on the mental health and wellbeing of adults who lived with domestic violence during their childhood.*

I can't really describe dad but I can describe the thoughts and feelings that I have held about him. I came to the conclusion a few years ago that I could describe him as 'the greatest horror of my life' for each time when my father shows up, that 'fight or flight' instinct kicks in, the adrenaline and cortisol stress hormones start pumping as I prepare for assault. Only one time I experienced physical assault aimed directly to me but many times to my mother, and therefore the fear of physical assault on top of verbal, social and emotional assault is real and remains. Plus the demands, the assumptions, the violation of space and privacy, the judgments, the criticisms, the lack of respect and understanding, the lack of love. Yes, I said it! "The lack of LOVE. " ☹

My father has always been interested in us but is very cold in the love and affection area and in recent years he would put his hand out to shake my hand on greeting me, and for me, hugging him was and still is very uncomfortable. It is almost as though he cannot differentiate between hugs of affection and lustful feelings so to avoid those feelings he will not hug his daughters. I suppose it's a protection for him and for us, and believe it or not, he has spoken on a number of occasions of his pride at not having had sex with any of his daughters. (This is an illustration of his thinking or maybe his affliction).

I often refer to the scene from the 1980's movie 'Jaws' to describe the feeling of terror when my dad appears without notice when we are in the midst of living our lives, and because he doesn't want to talk about it, his presence affects our calm and peace.

Picture the scene ….

'Families at the beach with the children playing in the sand, happily having a picnic lunch, joyful, relaxed, sunbathing on loungers and paddling and swimming in the sea, taking in some sunrays, Joie de vive.

Then suddenly, the sky blackens and the music plays – de-de, de-de, de-de de de De De DE DE… The music signifying the looming of the shark, the villain, the destroyer of joy, the killer, the enemy, the shark, JAWS!'

Everybody Scream!

Every time I think of it I equate it to my father's arrival, his 'pork pie' hat looming on the horizon, it can be seen before we realise that it is he.

Geraldine's Pearl by Marcia M

I am a grandmother now and my children even know to send warning signs to me if grandad pulls up outside or is on the telephone: they know the affect he can have on me still.

Early childhood trauma had a massive impact on my mental health and I grew up with intense anxiety, always having had this 'fearful feeling' in my stomach during which time, I would enter fight or flight all over again and until very recently, I found an answer to all of my ills: a deeper understanding of what we need to know to enjoy every aspect of life and I am thankful for this.

Geraldine's Pearl by Marcia M

Chapter Four

A Witness

Some of the incidents that I witnessed during my childhood were inclusive of waking in the morning and seeing the front room totally wrecked. This was traumatising for me on seeing my home in that state as it was totally confusing and distressing, hearing the domestic violence occurring, feeling the tension as we sat around the dining table. Even as a little girl I could sense trouble brewing and it frightened me.

Imagine being a little girl playing hopscotch in the back yard at about five or six years old and over your singing and skipping you can hear a strange sound coming from the house so you peep in through the back window of the house inquisitively to see what's happening. Oh my Gosh! Your eyes behold a horrifying scene, you see your father strangling your mother, you can see it happening and hear the noises, really strange noises, coming from your mother, as her neck and air pipes are being crushed as she struggles for breath, her limbs flailing, fighting for her life...

Geraldine's Pearl by Marcia M

...the little girl was frozen at that window, simply frozen in terror!

The scenes from my childhood come back in flashes, short flash-backs, previews or episodes. I'm not sure how they link together and where some of them begin or end. Hearing the sounds of violent attacks during the night and being paralysed with fear; how was I at my tender age to know what to do? My childhood was unstable to say the least, I wouldn't say dysfunctional because my mother did everything in her power to make a good life for us and to make us feel and be safe. The traumatic enduring of domestic violence lasted about five years, five long years of running away, living in rented rooms, staying with family to get away from our raging father. I reflect that my father was of a similar age as my son is now as I write and I cannot imagine my son raging like that and instilling fear in his child in such a way.

We were little children and we needed stability, me, my brother and our baby sister.

Geraldine's Pearl by Marcia M

Moving house was the norm for us, letting go of people and things; not really laying down any roots, we were 'travelling children' always in transition, a transient family, a family fighting for survival. My mother was supported by her mother and her family, whoever would give us refuge, we were almost like 'refugees' and running away was simply part of our 'normal'.

I have a clear recollection of getting up for school, dressing in my uniform and feeling so excited to go to school. I had loved school, at aged five or six years old I was very bright, very smart and eager to learn. But that morning I was disappointed, we were not going to school we were in fact moving away. Mom had devised a get-away plan to flee from the beast. He was and is bestial at times, the way that he drools when he eats: the way he beat, mishandled and forced himself onto my beautiful, delicate wonderful mother, was nothing but animalistic.

The thought of those scenes horrifies me therefore I will not go into detail for if I allowed my imagination to recreate those memories, the endurance of such hurt, the suffering, it would be too traumatising and a creation of my own mind and more likely not a true recollection.

In summary, my father's way of thinking has blighted maybe his life but most definitely the lives of his offspring in so much as we have had to endure the embarrassment of being 'his' children, the displays of pity from other family members, the humiliation of hearing family members recount their stories of incidents and conversations with him. He is often a hot topic of conversation, a person to ridicule and shame and to take the heat off themselves and their own misdemeanours.

This is because he really was different, eccentric, mad even. There were many times when I wanted to defend him against this disrespectful banter and then other times when I joined in and told some stories myself. I did sometimes find his stories and behaviour comical, ridiculous and entertaining conversation. He is the type of character who takes himself very seriously, he is larger than life, and he speaks things as he sees them and never fails to shock or offend.

Geraldine's Pearl by Marcia M

I feel that I do love him but I wish that he would be loveable; I wish that he could show me love and that he would be compassionate. My desire is for me to have the patience and thick skin to cope with his taunts of "You're a fool like your mother", "Only a fool would do such a thing" or "How much did you pay for that?" My father seems to be obsessed with money, sex and his sons. He has been quoted to say that if one of his daughters died it would not matter as he has more daughters. I think he speaks before he thinks about how it sounds, his mind tells him strange things and sometimes he just acts on them.

It is his belief that he is our 'righteous' father and that we must obey and respect him and it is this attitude that presents him with his frustration and bewilderment of the fact that many of his children are estranged from him by choice, his siblings also deliberately leaving him out of family gatherings for fear of his volatile unpredictable conduct.

Neville's jealousy and bitterness towards my step-father, for being there for his wife and children and grandchildren, did on

Geraldine's Pearl by Marcia M

rare occasions present itself through flashes of his enraged tongue.

Being Neville's children meant that we were socially isolated from our paternal family as those relatives did not stay in touch with us once our parents split. We were not invited to major family occasions including our grandparents' 'send- off', which was a large celebration afforded to people who actually achieved the dream and followed the plan of returning back home to Jamaica to retire. We were not even told when our father remarried, it appeared that our blood-line was severed, we were outcasts. We also have a beautiful and very intelligent younger sister by our father, Natalie, she is younger than my first child, it took many years until she was about eighteen, for her to be formally and finally introduced to us.

The only members of that large family who really showed any interest was my Uncle Eddy and his family, especially his daughter, my beloved cousin Liz. My relationship with Uncle Eddy is wonderful, I suppose he is the closest example of what my father could be like, if he could settle himself down. What

Geraldine's Pearl by Marcia M

I like about Uncle Eddy is that he speaks of my father with a love and respect that I do not hear from others, this is also reflected by Liz who is much like a sister, and by my youngest Uncle Bobby. It's a rare thing to find this and I truly value receiving positive viewpoints of dad who is ultimately that person from whom, my knowledge of self, my heritage, my identity is shaped.

Thank God again for my mother and her ability to give us a solid, secure foundation; I am truly thankful for this.

Chapter Five

The Sins of the Father – Learnt Behaviour

From what I understand from my Uncle Eddy and Liz, my father was very bright, with a real business brain, an entrepreneur and businessman and he was able to execute his ideas: in his thirties he owned four properties from which he made a good income. However, he was also a slave to his emotions, his moods, his paranoia, his thinking which would not always be in alignment with the truth. I relate to this very much so, like my father, I am an over-achiever, reaching milestones and achieving them at an early age but I too have had cause to manage my emotional health very carefully.

Dad was a womaniser, in fact he womanised alongside his own father and brothers in his early adulthood. Dad was very good looking, tall and broodingly silent, very attractive to many women; it was not difficult for him to woo them into bed.

Geraldine's Pearl by Marcia M

I once overheard, you know as children do, that my grandfather had a mistress for most of his years living in the UK. It seems that this was not a secret within the family as he and this wanton woman were not averse to flaunting their illicit and wicked relationship, whilst my quiet, down-trodden, disempowered grandmother Mary (who I realise now, that I did not know very well at all) would stay at home and go to church, keep house and just accept her husband's rules. Only recently I have learnt of my grandfather's physical and mental violence towards my grandmother, this didn't surprise me but rather I was disappointed.

I knew as a child that she was oppressed, I sensed it even though I did not have the words to define it and secretly, I despised grandad for this, I could see and feel the injustice. You know as a child growing up we were to be 'seen and not heard', well I learnt so much as a child by being quiet, being there and absorbing a whole gamut of information. I often decided on which side I would take, I was always a hater of injustice and a lover of children and women. I grew with a disdain for men and their actions and choices, and of the impact on their children especially.

Apparently Mary had been given by her father to an older man, she was sent to be a house-help but the man took advantage of her and she bore a child by him in her mid-teens. Some years later she met my grandfather, they married and she bore him eight children, the first birth was to twin boys, however one of the twins named Lionel died at or close to their birth. I will reconnect with this story later.

I know that my grandfather would not have allowed my grandmother to ever forget her humble beginnings and would use it as a method of disempowerment, control and abuse.

My grandfather was a 'bellowing' man with a booming, deep bass voice. He was way over 6ft tall and he loved himself, he was well groomed, fair skinned with soft wavy hair. He had a good job, a large property, a flashy car, a Rover, and he could get the women, and he was afraid of no-one and would fight anyone if he had to. He was confident and powerful William!!!

Geraldine's Pearl by Marcia M

He was a man's man and loved by the ladies, a man who demanded and commanded respect. As a child I decided that I didn't like him. What made me dislike him was from two stories related to the domestic violence that my mother had endured and survived at the hands of his son, his son who modelled his lifestyle from his father's example.

There was an incident when my father had badly beaten my mother and she was covered in bruises and had to run for help, as always taking us with her. My maternal grandfather and uncle decided to go to see my paternal grandfather to reason with him about the beatings that his son was inflicting on my mother. As the story goes, I believe that William rolled up his sleeves making ready to fight my mother's family, as though he was defending the abhorrent behaviour, but I suppose he would as he had been my father's role model.

Dad holds a strong affinity to his father and his father's ideals, it is as though he wants to be just like him and he attempts to replicate William's characteristics and traits. Whilst William was able to rule his sons even into their sixties, I have

Geraldine's Pearl by Marcia M

witnessed him dominate and control his sons on many an occasion. Neville, however, lost his grip on his children, the little respect that we had for him died years ago and he is frustrated and bewildered by this. He tries to bribe us with money, mistakenly, as money is not our motivator. The bribes do not work on us to encourage us to spend more than is necessary time with him for our respect and loyalty cannot be bought.

The second incident was when my family had moved from Birmingham to North Wales. Our father was a Diamond Cutter, Jewellery Engraver and I was approximately eight years of age at the time. It's unbelievable that some memories from that long ago are still so vivid; my dad must have been about thirty years of age. We were moved to North Wales in 1975 and we were the only Black family in the region and at our school – (I will tell you more about being a Black child in Wales later.)

Geraldine's Pearl by Marcia M

The domestic abuse was heightened whist living in Wales, my mother pregnant and subsequently giving birth to her youngest daughter Leona, in Wales. Mom was totally isolated from her family. My father, feeling and acting like he was a super stud, we had a good income, nice modern home and he was the only Black man around. Yet again he was popular with the women and proceeded with his womanising behaviour, charming and bedding whosoever he chose, alongside the physical, psychological, sexual and financial abuse he subjected my mother to. "I don't like dad" I used to think, he changed moods so suddenly, at times we could really feel the strain in the house: poor mom, I think now. But Olive was a fighter and she was a protector! Hurray!

One night we were in bed and I heard a violent scene erupting with banging, crashing, cries. It was awful and it was terrifying, lying in bed at eight years of age, frozen for a moment but the noises were not stopping and the violence did not cease. I was scared but I knew that we needed help, I thought about what I needed to do, using my wits and common sense.

Geraldine's Pearl by Marcia M

I proceeded to go down the stairs and out of the front door, leaving my siblings asleep, I think they were asleep. I ran over to our neighbour's front door and knocked and knocked, I asked them to help us and fortunately they responded. They got my mother out and the other children. This was part of a series of episodes, during which time I was traumatised and felt very unsafe, I felt at a constant risk of danger, I was terrified about what my father would do next. The fear of harm and danger can be even more terrifying than the actual act itself, my fears for my mom, my siblings and my own safety had me wracked with anxiety at such a tender age.

I recall deciding to take action to get us away from Dad, I remember taking change out of my father's jacket pocket that was hanging in the hallway, somehow I had memorised my paternal grandparents' telephone number. I was in rural North Wales and they were in Handsworth Birmingham. I walked to the telephone box, in my desperate attempt to save us. We needed help. I dialled the number and after a short time of ringing my aunt answered. I was relieved. I pushed the

Geraldine's Pearl by Marcia M

money into the slot quickly, I do not remember what I said to her but I know that I begged for them to help us.

At a later date many years after this, my aunt who is only five years older than me, shared that she still feels chills when her mind goes back to that call: she said I was pleading for our lives saying "Come and help us, please come and get us, he's going to kill us!" On hearing this I was stunned and the memories and tears came flooding back. I think I had asked for my grandfather, I think I spoke to him, I was eight years of age fighting for the life of my mother, my siblings and myself, begging and pleading with my family for help! By the way, he didn't come, he didn't help, he didn't respond to my pleas.

Chapter Six

School Life

In our early years we were cared for by our grandmothers, Adam by Grandma Mary and me by Gong Gong. I also went to Nursery School and Gong Gong would collect me and take me to the laundrette where she worked briefly. I attended seven different primary schools during my childhood and thankfully one secondary school. The first school in Handsworth that we attended was St James Church of England and I remember drinking warm milk (sun temperature) through straws from bottles with cream on the top. It was OK, I suffered it, but Adam really didn't like it. Adam also once got into trouble for stabbing a girl with his pencil. He was four years old. That's it – that's my memories of that school experience.

We had a disrupted and fractured early education experience, because of the midnight escapes, daily drama and trauma. Grief, loss, bereavement, trauma, fear, paralysis with shock, lack of control, terror, helplessness, denial, misunderstood, overlooked, unsupported, neglected, refugees. We were

Geraldine's Pearl by Marcia M

travelling transient children and we were refugees, my mother would have to seek refuge for us in rented rooms and on sofas and spaces within our extended family's homes.

My memories of school - I loved school, it was my place of escape from the drama, and I was very bright, an all -round gifted and talented child. I was creative, confident and agile; I could sing, dance, read well and could write. I was a high achiever, an over-achiever and against the backdrop of my nomadic home life, I did well at every school, I stood out, I made an impression.

School was the beginning of my default strategy, the place where I was able to put aside my pains and just indulge myself in learning, creating, developing and performing. I was physically and mentally strong, socially I was quite popular, I had friends even though I always felt outside of the group, I felt different, removed, alone but not necessarily lonely. My resilience and life experiences had given me an internal ability to find strength from within. At the age of nine years I knew that I depended on me, I knew about responsibility, I felt a strong sense of care and duty towards my family, my mom and my younger siblings.

We were loved by our extended families but I just feel that they often did not know what to say or do to console us or help in our circumstances. I have since learnt that it takes skill, confidence and a deeper knowledge of the sociological and psychological effects on children living in domestic abuse households to be able to comfort them and facilitate healing. However, having said that, one of the pre-determining factors for healing was that there was LOVE, we were also given something much more soothing than refuge, we were afforded sanctuary, a safe space to rest a little while in between weathering the storm again; it is commonplace in the cycle of domestic abuse for the perpetrator to woo the victim back into the relationship and then the cycle turns again, leading to an escalation of the violence and terror.

What was this chapter about? Oh yes school life, I forget, as you see my childhood memories are dominated by the

Geraldine's Pearl by Marcia M

domestic abuse and violence, the transient existence, the refugee status, so much so, that my memories are clouded.

We attended two schools in Bristol as we fled to my maternal great Aunt's home on a number of occasions, we were given sanctuary within a family that was so large it was bursting at the seams, and they were rich with and still are, with love.

Residing with our Aunt Brenda and Uncle Geoff with the family who at the time in the early 70's were eight children and eighteen grandchildren and the four of us, mom and her three children, was awesome. I have no idea where we slept at all. Now, forty years later I visit that house and see that it was a small two-bedroom terrace, I reiterate, I really don't remember where we slept but I do remember the love and the feeling of safety where we could just be children and relax a little. Whilst in Bristol we also stayed at my grandmother's brother's home and in rented rooms. I still can't recall much about school but I can tell you about two significant incidents that occurred whilst living there in Bristol.

Geraldine's Pearl by Marcia M

As I stated earlier, we lived in rented rooms in a shared house, myself, mom, Adam and Amanda. We had two rooms for our family, a living space and a bedroom, and a woman lived downstairs and we shared the kitchen, I believe. This was in the early '70's and in those days it was accepted/tolerated for parents to leave their children at home when they went out and even whilst they worked.

On that particular day, myself and Adam were playing in our rooms that were heated by a paraffin lamp, which was a form of heating that was commonplace in that era, the lamp stood tall in the middle of the living room. I was playing and suddenly as I accidentally ran into the lamp, both of my legs stuck to the lamp. It's really strange that as I landed on top of the lamp, my legs fastened to the hot metal by my melted skin and flesh, I had landed on the lamp yet my buttocks and vagina did not get burnt.

The woman downstairs heard my shrill screams from her living space downstairs, she ran up to see what had caused me to cry out like that and on entering the room she found

Geraldine's Pearl by Marcia M

me burnt, writhing and screaming with pain, having burnt myself from the tops of my inner thighs to my knees on both legs. Trying to help she applied butter to the burns. Oh My Gosh! The burns began to fry; I was in even more pain. The pain was intense, insufferable; I was then rushed to the Accident and Emergency Department, my mom meeting me there. It's all a bit of a blur now but I remember crying out "Jesus, Jesus" over and over again, "Jesus help me!"

Those burns were awful and I had to wear bandages and gauze dressings for months as they healed slowly and sometimes the gauze or the bandages would get stuck to my weeping flesh or even my trousers and the only way to remove them was to rip them off, well I think that was the only way, at least that's the way it was done. Oh the pain, the pain; this is my most vivid memory of Bristol, as I said before, I really don't have much recollection of school there but I know that we attended two different ones at different times.

Geraldine's Pearl by Marcia M

My second significant memory is of dad coming to where we were staying, intent in his efforts to reconcile with his wife and children and encourage her to come back. I mean in his mind he only slapped her and he felt that it was nothing, that it was acceptable; but he promised that he would change; he promised that he would get help if she came back and the cycle continued again and again.

We returned to Handsworth and were duly registered to begin at the Rookery Road School, a busy, vibrant and colourful place of learning, with loads of Black and Asian children. We had fun, I used to sing, was good at P.E., in those days we participated in P.E. wearing only our pants and vests. I was well on track to achieve the 11+ when I reached that age or so they predicted.

I cherished my memories of walking to school with my cousin Mo, and she was one of my first real friends. Mo was run over by a car around that time and this was very worrying for me but thankfully she made a full recovery. We were unable to

Geraldine's Pearl by Marcia M

maintain our friendship because of the many house moves that my family made.

Our next move was to North Wales, deep in the valleys, and this experience was different in that we moved as a whole family. We attended school in the centre of Corwen. I was in Standard 1, that's what they called the years, and I think my brother was in the same class. We, as children from England, had to learn to speak Welsh so we were taught in special classes to learn the language. I learnt quickly and I was adept at picking up the language fast. I did so well that I was able to eloquently recite poetry speaking in the Gaelic Welsh language thus I was entered into an Eisteddfod, which is a Welsh celebration of arts and culture. I recited a poem called "Y Bus", ("The Bus").

I mostly remember the fights that we had as Black children. With the blatant racism in the mid 70's, we were asked questions like "Is your shit white?", "Do you come from a jungle?" and being called 'nigger' as the kids taunted us with chants like "Nigger, Nigger sleep in the jungle naked!"

It was quite shocking. We had always lived in the inner cities and attended schools with a substantial number of children from Caribbean and Asian heritages. I hadn't experienced this type of racially verbal assault before, it was confusing. Yet it was ok, I could defend myself either with my razor sharp tongue or I would just use my fist and beat them up. It was simply self-defence. There were times when I and my siblings were fighting together, we would be surrounded by a large group of White children, looking at us and jeering us on, but we soon put them in their place. If someone started on Amanda, Adam would jump in to defend her and then if needed, I would join in. It wasn't long before they retreated and left us alone, either the novelty wore off or they were just too scared to test us and we soon made friends, we even had best friends and integrated into the community.

Wales was heavenly, lush and green, loads of open spaces, trees to climb, freedom to play and explore, we enjoyed the

Geraldine's Pearl by Marcia M

outdoors, went on long treks, sometimes with and without our parents. We would pick berries, apples and my favourite hazelnuts fresh from the tree - delicious. It was idyllic, living in the valleys, in the Welsh countryside - awesome!

My parents also invested in me having horse-riding lessons, an amazing experience, even the times when I fell off the horse when she bolted. Her name was Talia. You see my mom never ceased to invest in her children's development, my mom Olive is amazing.

Chapter Seven

Family

When our parents separated for the final time and we had moved back to Birmingham, we then changed schools again to attend a Catholic Primary School, local to our grandparents' home where we were staying in Oldbury. Yet again we had to settle in part way through the academic year. I was then nine years of age approaching ten. I had a vivid imagination, I had read many, many books, and I read every night to get me to sleep. I wrote stories at home and in class and I recall that in my mind I saw my character as a White girl. I didn't want to be white but I believe that as all of the books that I had read the characters were White, on television the characters were White, therefore in my mind, when I imagined a story, every character including myself was White. WOW!

I made some good friends at this school; I think I was there for about a year. The school was quite cosmopolitan and my friends were Polish and Italian, although yet again, I felt on the outside of our group, I always felt distant, an outsider, a

Geraldine's Pearl by Marcia M

loner, different. I was a leader I know, I felt somehow set apart. I held strong opinions about life and had vast and varied life experiences and had been through tests socially and emotionally. I was also developing physically and I had reached puberty, my breast buds had grown and my menses came when I was ten years old. I was growing up! I recall telling my mom "I think I've started to menstruate." My mom, in recent years, said she giggled at the way I used the correct and full word for starting my periods but that the proper words was all I knew. I had read about them in the family encyclopaedia.

Between school in Wales and school in Oldbury, came the life-changing choices that my mother made. Yes, I am talking about domestic abuse and violence again and its effects, I have no choice but to speak of it as it dominated my formative years and those of my brother and our little sister Amanda, albeit maybe to a lesser degree for Amanda as she was much younger.

Geraldine's Pearl by Marcia M

Chapter Eight

Game Changer - Life Changer!

That Easter weekend, in North Wales, we were in a place of refuge, staying with neighbours in their house a few doors away from ours, whisked away from 'home' (home that is meant to be your sanctuary,) to another location of safety, bewildered yet again, three traumatised young children and a baby, in unsettled, unstable circumstances over which they had no control. It was at this time I had called my grandfather and during this time that I had run out of the door and knocked for help for rescue. I felt that we needed to be rescued and finally rescue came and we were moved back to Birmingham, finally what I had been trying to influence had been achieved and at long last, adults had to intervene as I was an eight year- old girl who was powerless to completely resolve the situation.

We were welcomed into my maternal grandmother's home, a bustling, busy place with my aunts and uncles and cousins. I loved being at my grandma's house. Grandma was a strong

Geraldine's Pearl by Marcia M

matriarch, she was busy managing her household and she was an excellent manager, a leader, an organiser, a strategic planner and a skilled entrepreneur. At the time that we lived at my maternal grandparents' home there too lived four aunts, one uncle, two cousins and we four children and our mom, that was five of us plus grandma and grandad - a total of fourteen people in a three- bedroom house.

The house had two living rooms downstairs, one being a typical front room that we didn't use very often and the main living space where we sat together and watched T.V. Children had to sit on the floor if the adults were present, and my grandmother's sewing machine, a dining table and a large sofa occupied the rest of the room. Grandma enforced a really effective regime of set meals each day, shopping days, laundry days etc. Everyone had a role to play in the mechanics of Gong Gong's family household, we all had chores/ jobs to complete and one of mine was washing up and rinsing so we worked in pairs as one washed and the other rinsed the dishes in a basin that was placed on a chair beside the sink. I also had to dust the skirting boards every Saturday. My aunts, except

Geraldine's Pearl by Marcia M

Aunt Patricia, who was the youngest, were all adults in their twenties and as some of them contributed to or covered the household bills, everything was well organised and executed.

Where did we all sleep? This still baffles me; at times I shared a double bed with the boys, Micky, Chris & Adam, with baby Leona in the cot next to us. I think Amanda slept with one or two of our aunts. I, to this day, have no idea where our mom slept and in all these years since I have never asked her - perhaps I should, I think I will or she may even tell me after reading this book.

My memories of the several months that we lived at my maternal grandma's are some of my fondest, we had loads of fun with our cousins and we got up to a great deal of mischief. Oh the joys of childhood and family! We were safe, loved and relaxed. Initially, I was very angry with my father but that subsided as I became absorbed in probably the best time of my childhood.

Geraldine's Pearl by Marcia M

In the long six weeks' summer holidays, we were out ALL day, like wild children. I was a boisterous tomboy, skilled at riding my bicycle free-handed; I could climb trees and run very fast. I taught the boys how to ride their bikes, I was the leader of the pack as Grandma many times had called me the 'ringleader' when she scolded us and would chase us off calling us "A generation of vipers". These memories make me giggle as I now realise that her scolding was all with love from my precious, fastidious grandmother whom we fondly called 'Gong Gong'.

Life was good and on Friday nights grandad would come home from the pub, bringing us a treat of smoky bacon crisps or even Kentucky fried chicken (KFC). I think of my poor angelic Aunty Patricia, only four years my senior, who had to share her parents with us. Aunty Pat didn't really play with us, maybe because we were too wild, we had different upbringings, we had all come from broken relationships where as she was the 'wash belly' of our grandparents, their special baby, their youngest child.

Geraldine's Pearl by Marcia M

We went to Sunday school every week, this was a tradition that mom made sure of, in fact everywhere we lived we went to Sunday school and I developed a deep and steadfast faith and belief in Jesus. As a child, Jesus was my saviour, it was Jesus who I turned to in my times of need and I could rely on Jesus. Although I wasn't a saint by any means and still in this present day I am not, I have always been God-fearing and God-loving, I have always been aware of a love from a higher place beyond any human.

Chapter Nine

Grandmother's Influence

My grandmother's home was a wonderful place. She was an amazing woman, powerful and strong in her faith in Jesus Christ, her Lord and Saviour. The front room was testament to this as she held regular prayer meetings with her brethren from church, praying and seeking God. I understand this now but as a child it was a lot of loud noises, shouting, jumping and banging. It was a bit scary to listen to at first but then we just got used to it as it was part of the atmosphere of this Godly home.

My uncle was an Actor and he travelled the world, his sons lived at grandmas; their mother had emigrated to Canada. Broken-hearted, I share this story as it was very poignant and as a little girl I felt the pain of all parties involved and it was a tragic story. My observation was of my cousins who lived without regular contact with their mother or father. Whilst grandma and grandad were fantastic, my strong sense of

Geraldine's Pearl by Marcia M

injustice and my awareness that children needed their parents could not stop me from feeling over protective for my cousins. I found it difficult to understand why they seemed to have no parents. I could see and feel their pain and their daily struggles and I wished many a time that I could make it right. I took responsibility to look out for their welfare and to check on the adults to make sure that they did right by them. I was nine years old.

We were all displaced children who had found sanctuary in our grandma's love and she would stand us all up by her bed and teach us The Bible. Grandma was a Sunday School Teacher. Ensuring that she taught her own grand-children before going to teach her class at church, we learnt the 'golden text' and I was taught recitations, we were taught songs and I loved Jesus, I loved church and really loved grandma. Not to say grandma was easy because she was tough and strict, she didn't mince her words, she was direct, she gave my mother and her sisters a hard time, and I remember that. On reflection I see that she was leading and directing, she wanted the best for her girls, she wanted them

Geraldine's Pearl by Marcia M

to be safe and she wanted to guard their modesty and reputation so therefore she raised them to be ladies. A lot of this training also influenced my upbringing, although I must admit, I am not as lady-like as my wonderful mother and aunts; I'm too much of a tomboy.

Grandma came across as controlling, she had to be in charge, things must go her way, but in hindsight, I now believe that she was probably a very anxious person, she trusted God and relied on him to guide and protect. Grandma prayed for us all on her knees by her bedside every morning and every night, I'm sure that she even prayed silently for us throughout the day. She wanted the best for us all and she covered us all with her prayers by naming us one by one. Imagine every morning and every night for forty-four years she prayed for me and as she aged, she was unable to get on her knees but never the less, she prayed.

Her faith made her strong, her faith kept her going, her faith kept me going and her faith made me strong. Halleluiah!

Geraldine's Pearl by Marcia M

What I am beginning to realise since her death is that I had no choice but to be a strong woman, my genetics alone from my grandmother and mother afforded me strength, afforded me vision, tenacity and leadership qualities. From both of these women I inherited the true value and meaning of mothering, of nurturing and of kindness. Both virtuous women, I have seen my grandmother many, many times help others who were less fortunate than herself. She gave a charitable hand to others all of her life and for me, charity equals love. Grandma gave for nothing in return; she gave just to give, to bless another and loved to help and to assist others.

Grandma was what I now call a Community Philanthropist, she invested time, energy, talents and finances, not forgetting food and clothing, into others, and she also invested heavily into her church. Grandma, 'Mother Gee', was a leader in her church community, developing projects and initiatives, fundraising, teaching, advising and giving. She was blessed with the gift of extending her kindness and help to others. For me, that was the very essence of a Grandma, that's what they

Geraldine's Pearl by Marcia M

do, that's who they are, and they are women who are strong in love.

I am not saying that Grandma had no weaknesses for she clearly did, but I believe that is where her faith came in and she would lean on Christ as her comfort and protector: "On Christ the solid rock I stand", she would sing "I have Christ what want I more". Grandma's handbag contained her Bible and her hymnal. Grandma was a songstress, a beautiful soprano voice she had, and she sang in the choir and sang solo for many years. I was very proud of her. "My Grandma, my Gong Gong", she made me proud and honoured to be her grand-daughter and I was her extra special first grandchild.

Chapter Ten

Wonder Woman

What I am realising now though is that my mother has always been my super role model, she is THE wonder woman. I do recall when I was twenty-one, declaring my admiration of my mother by saying "If I could be half the woman my mother is, I would be a great woman". My mother never allowed her circumstances to ruin her life; she has a fire inside her that makes her so attractive for one but so full of hope, full of the joys of life. Mom fought her way through domestic abuse and domestic violence and she reminded me that she fought back, physically and mentally, she overcame my father in many ways and executed adept survival strategies for herself and her children.

Then after nine years, she got away and built an amazing life for herself by making wise choices and despite having four children she was able to take the greatest revenge and that was success!

Geraldine's Pearl by Marcia M

Olive is the first child born to Gee, reared by her grandparents and was brought to the UK at the age of sixteen years-old. The elders in my life were simply wonderful, my mom, my grandma, my Aunt Brenda and my Godmother Aunt Melissa, who was the happiest woman alive.

The actions of men and women have influenced my outlook on life, the network of women in our family who pulled together to raise us was a phenomenally, well-orchestrated team who carried the weight of someone in their family or community when they were in need. I grew up being raised around these impactful women who invested the little that they had into the interests of others. My grandma hardly worked outside of the home yet her life had true meaning and purpose, she held a high standing in her community and church, initiating and leading on many projects alongside raising children and grandchildren.

I too witnessed my mother involving herself in community and educational activism and then going on to study at university at the age of forty and building a solid career in Social Work so

Geraldine's Pearl by Marcia M

that on her early retirement, she was a Manager in a Fostering Team. These women knew how to keep going even when the going got tough and they battled and prayed through it. When someone needed money it was not unusual for individuals to 'put' towards raised funds to make up the money, that's how they operated.

Chapter Eleven

Olive and Mike

Olive looked at herself in the mirror and looked straight into her eyes and that fire in her belly told her that she was worth more, that she deserved a better life than the one she was subjected to and that she could and would get away. "Maas Hues grand-pickney can't be abused anymore!" She asserted to herself.

So she fought with her whole might, her whole spirit, her faith, her strength, her self-belief and she fought her way out of the abuse with her four babies, she fought for her life and finally was FREE!!!! The separation and ensuing divorce was not easy, Olive had four children to provide for whilst initially staying with her parents before they moved to rented council accommodation, her own place with her children, a three-bedroom maisonette in West Bromwich. There were times when dad would turn up causing a little disruption to the peace and harmony of the new home that mom had created.

Geraldine's Pearl by Marcia M

Mom met Mike, a White male, in his twenties and living with his parents: they met and fell in love, and they dated for a couple of years and then married. 'Mom and Mike' - my parents, built the strongest marriage relationship that I have ever observed. They as a team were excellent parents. We, particularly Adam and I, were children with complex needs so they could be forgiven for not understanding my sometimes 'acting out' behaviour and Adam's 'quiet shyness'.

Mom getting together with Mike was a tenuous, dichotomy of emotions of comfort and discomfort. I reflect that this man came into our lives and was someone that I used to sit beside at the age of ten and hug, he was very huggable, it was a lovely feeling, he was slightly overweight and that made him very cuddly. I do not recall having hugged my father or any man like that before then for that matter. Mike was a cuddly teddy bear, and I felt protected and safe with my arms around him. It was also a frightening experience as yet again change was upon us and I had no say or control over what was ensuing for me and my siblings.

Geraldine's Pearl by Marcia M

I was the child who had witnessed much injustice and unfairness and I strongly felt that children should have a voice; I was mature, yet too immature to really grasp and balance understanding of everything that was happening. At times I felt we could have been consulted more about our fears, our wishes and our feelings. I used to have tantrums when I was afraid, when I did not understand and I would stamp and shout in protest. Having said that, Mom did make the right and proper decisions for herself and her brood and along with Mike, they built a beautiful life and a successful marriage, they created wonderful memories for us and for our children plus new opportunities for my children and my grandchildren with their new home in Europe.

I felt that I loved Mike but also felt a struggle to get close to mom. At times my heart ached as though he had taken her from me, I mean mom and I had been through so much together, the terror and the running; picking up the pieces, the continuous displacements and our fight for survival. We went through it together and now she had someone else by her side. I don't know if mom realised this and I also know that this was when life was settling down.

Mom had Mike and that was great, but I struggled as I could see that Mike did not have the capacity to appreciate our needs, for at the time he was very young and inexperienced. We had been through so much in our formative years and needed someone extra special, who had patience and empathy, and we didn't even understand ourselves that we may have symptoms of Post-Traumatic Stress Disorder or similar emotional and psychological scars. Mike was very patient and sensitive I think, but against the backdrop of his stable, settled childhood it would have been difficult for him to comprehend our situation.

Previously I spoke of my father having mental health issues: we definitely inherited a propensity to develop a mental health issue, we inherited depression, we probably were a little depressed as children but then we could just about get away with crying a lot; however, as adults it was different. At different points in all of our lives the depression manifested, when the heat was turned up our vulnerability to breaking down was illuminated.

We faced challenges when I reached my defiant teenage years, during which I suffered, (as do millions of teenagers), a real identity crisis. At secondary school we were teased by black children asking us if we ate beans on toast for dinner - I was a Black girl being mistaken for a mixed race girl. I had light skin and soft hair but I was Black, I was Black, I was Black! It was uncomfortable at home to assert our Black identity, we were scolded for speaking anything like Jamaican Patois, we were also thrust into a new family, a White family, with mom adopting some of the traditions such as having 'tea' in the evenings, until the novelty wore off, but I found it distressing, a struggle, being a teenager was confusing enough let alone being mistaken for a different identity.

This is not disrespect to people of mixed heritage or white people but if you are NOT something then you simply are NOT! I am Black!

Geraldine's Pearl by Marcia M

I was drawn to mixing with the black children at secondary school as I should, I needed people that I identified with, and I needed people grounded in the identity that I felt that I was losing or maybe had lost due to circumstances.

At eleven years of age I had soft, shoulder length hair that would be scooped up into clips and elastics and plaits. I sometimes wore my hair in a bun or straightened it yet for some strange reason my mother and my stepfather decided that I should have my hair cut really short like a boy. They had seen a woman in a magazine that looked really stunning with short hair and felt that that would be better for me to save having to manage it on a daily basis. I went along with the idea, I had no choice. I didn't like it! It didn't make sense, it went against black culture that when everyone was busy trying to grow and lengthen their hair, mine was chopped off! "A violation"! Very strange, very difficult being a short haired girl when you previously had a head of beautiful hair.

High school days were OK: my mom fought an appeal to get me into where was considered to be the best school in the

Geraldine's Pearl by Marcia M

area. Then when I was twelve years of age, mom and Mike married and the self-identity crisis and battles with my stepfather ensued, he was a great husband and a good father to my younger siblings but for me there was always a distance, a miscommunication, an emotional gap. I was still struggling with my identity; I also lived many miles from the school, in a different town. We had no roots in the town of Walsall where we now lived, not that we really had roots in West Bromwich where our school was either, we'd had such a nomadic existence that we really didn't seem to belong anywhere.

I think that growing up, I always felt alone and lonely, I was different and set apart from my peers. As ever, I was in top sets for everything, I was able academically; I was one of the few black children in this position in my school. I also sang in the school choir and was given solo parts in concerts and shows; I have a soprano voice, soft and delicate. I represented the school in every sport including trampoline, swimming, netball, hockey, rounders and athletics. I swiftly became the school's and Sandwell's champion athlete at the

Geraldine's Pearl by Marcia M

age of thirteen and fourteen, receiving national recognition in the newspapers for my abilities.

I stopped playing team sports and focussed on my individual performance, this is where the real signs of me being an eagle began to show, I was not and never will be a groupie, not a chicken, not part of a pack or group. I was independent, a leader and I was often lonely. I also did public speaking and drama – yes, I was most definitely a gifted and talented pupil. I didn't realise this then, it is only as I write that I can give myself this validation, back then I did not know who I was.

I would say I was a pretty girl and by the age of fourteen I had a fit and athletic body and I was clever. These factors, I have learnt over the years, made me attractive to many boys and boys of all nations: Black, White and Asian boys declared their attraction to me, their admiration even, some only told me many years later when we were adults. But I only liked Black boys, dark skinned black boys. I started having boyfriends at the age of fourteen. I had an overwhelming crush on a slightly older boy at school, I think he was sixteen, and we said that

Geraldine's Pearl by Marcia M

we were 'going out' with each other. We would speak on the telephone and we used to kiss under the subway after school, this was my first crush, my first love.

It's funny looking back but it was an important first step towards a relationship and the awakening of real adult sexuality as we did kiss a lot whenever we were together. Many months later I spent time with another boy who skilfully took my virginity, he knew what he was doing and he executed his mission to take that thing, it was a bit of a non-event to be honest but it happened, I had done it, I had had sex! Once!

Geraldine's Pearl by Marcia M

Chapter Twelve

Love Story and Heart-Break

I was on the bus on my way to athletics training, it was mid July 1983 and I was exactly fifteen years and six months old. At the time I was running for Warley Harriers and the journey to the stadium involved two buses, one to West Bromwich and the other to Smethwick. This meant that I passed through West Bromwich Town a few evenings each week as training was 6pm to 8pm which meant that I would get home for about 9.30pm on each of those evenings.

On that particular evening, I saw him. I was sitting at the top of the double decker bus and I looked down and there he was - dark chocolate brown, he was different to the other boys, he was older. I saw him running for the bus and I silently but fervently willed him to catch the bus. This is the day that I met the love of my life. (Even thirty-three years later as I write, tears come to my eyes for the sadness of our love story).

Geraldine's Pearl by Marcia M

What can I tell you about this person and the true love that we shared? I will use his name, Vince. I liked the look of him because he appeared different, I liked that, it excited me. He caught the bus and came upstairs. Oh my gosh! He had an amazingly cheeky smile, warm and very sexy; he was on his way home from work, eighteen years old and a man. I was still at school. He was exciting and we had a chat on the bus. I told him that I was going training and he asked me "Do you wanna meet me for a drink after?" Well, I couldn't resist so "Yes" I replied softly. "Wow" I thought "He's nice".

So we met afterwards and from that day we were inseparable: he was my boyfriend, we loved each other, and we went out together, visited each other's homes, we were together and really deeply, madly in love, really in love. It was just one of those situations when you just know that you are in love with someone and that they feel equally the same about you. It was amazing, out of this world, we became branded as 'the couple of West Bromwich' as we would be seen holding hands everywhere.

Geraldine's Pearl by Marcia M

Vince and my relationship was solid, the love was there, he was an extrovert, warm and loving, his kiss was heavenly and we were compatible in many ways. Our backgrounds were in complete contrast. I am of Jamaican heritage from a large family, my parents divorced and I was step-parented, my mom was a professional working in Social Work and my stepfather was White. Vince's parents came from the Windward Islands, St Vincent and the Grenadines and Caricou. Vince's mom had mental health needs, therefore his sister and his father ran the home, a very clean home, a place that I visited very often, to the point where it became my second home.

We gradually integrated into each other's families as our love was true, a true romance. We would go out to eat, to drink in wine bars, walks in the park, in the town simply spending time together. I really loved Vince and I had found the love and security that I had yearned for, and in return he loved me. He was well groomed and he dressed immaculately and at the time my friends called him 'trash and ready!' - meaning super dapper with lots of swagger. He was sexy, fun, sporty, tough

Geraldine's Pearl by Marcia M

and strong and he was mine and I was his: you know that feeling when your heart is entwined with another, that feeling that you just belong together - that was us. Subconsciously I believe that I'd always wanted to be with someone who was tough enough to stand up to my dad if necessary, someone who could protect me and it seems that these were the type of men that I attracted and more to the point that I was attracted to. Vince was a brilliant footballer and he also was a fighter. Despite his slight frame he could handle himself, often times he found himself in scrapes on the football terraces as he supported our local team, West Bromwich Albion, in his terms he loved a 'row'. So I felt safe in his company that no harm would come to me.

When I was seventeen, if my parents didn't hear from me they would know that I was at his flat. I loved the very essence of him, his scent, his skin, the fire in his eyes. At the time I was at college studying travel and tourism and it was a glamorous job with a cute uniform. I spent all of my spare time with Vinnie, as we affectionately called him, and I didn't have close female friends.

Geraldine's Pearl by Marcia M

I was pregnant at the age of seventeen and I didn't have that baby. We thought that I was too young, I lived with my parents, it wasn't right, but it was heart-breaking for both of us. It's a particular heart-break because only a year later I fell pregnant again with our son Solomon, who was born just ten days after my nineteenth birthday. Solomon is the second love of my life. Solomon was a child born out of love, the love of two people who never wanted to be apart, who were dedicated to one another and believed that they would be together forever.

I had left home as soon as I reached eighteen. I was spending so much of my time with the love of my life that it seemed to make sense to give it a try. I told my parents that I was going to live with Vince for a trial period and my stepfather responded with "Why don't you go for good?" I was a little surprised and taken aback by his response, but go for good I did.

I was working in a Travel Agency and arrived at work vomiting on a few mornings. The first time it happened I had thought

Geraldine's Pearl by Marcia M

that it was the Chinese takeaway that we had eaten the night before but after a couple of occurrences and my missed period, I contemplated that I might really be pregnant. As it proved to be, I sure was. I telephoned my mother from work to tell her. I was so nervous that as soon as she answered I blurted out "Mom, I'm pregnant" and her immediate response was "Well get married then".

Vince and I had been planning to get engaged that year so to me it seemed OK to consider marrying. You see, my mother had had to get married when she was expecting me, this was also true for some of her sisters and now it appeared that it was my turn for what people call a 'shotgun wedding'. This was an attempt to by-pass the shame and disgrace of illegitimate children being born, to make it look better. I believe that for my grandmother this was vitally important as she felt some shame or was made to feel ashamed when she was pregnant and out of wedlock with my mother.

Vince and I were in love so we didn't mind whatever was decided, we were simply excited for our forthcoming child. So

Geraldine's Pearl by Marcia M

we began our plans to get married, an inferior wedding at the local registry office and a meal at my uncle's restaurant. My mom had influenced every step of the wedding and I went along with it. She decided that we would not invite children which meant that my closest cousin couldn't attend - it made **no** sense to me but I was only eighteen years of age, still a child myself.

My mom chose my wedding outfit, a peach dress and a cream hat; I think it was one of my grandma's church hats. It was a beautiful dress and I still have it to this day. But it was not really what I wanted but I went along with it. I don't think I really knew what I wanted in life back then as I was sort of lost in my emotions and had never really thought about any dreams or aspirations; my main pursuit in life was to feel safe and loved with an element of security and stability. Unlike many other girls, I hadn't dreamt of the wedding or the dress or anything like that, to be honest.

My 'shame' was covered, although I wasn't ashamed as I was with the love of my life and we were having our blessed child.

I then became engrossed in buying baby equipment, researching and studying about birth and baby care. I read to increase my knowledge, because even though we didn't have a great deal of money, we acquired all of the essentials that our child would need.

Chapter Thirteen

Motherhood

The night I went into labour my mother was away on training, studying Social Work, this was two weeks before my due date. I had ballooned from eight stones to twelve stones and I developed very high blood pressure. My waters broke yet I hadn't felt a thing. Vince went to the telephone box and called Mike, my stepfather, and he and my younger brother came and drove us to the hospital.

So this was labour: so far no pain, just water leaking everywhere. On arrival at the hospital I was ushered into the maternity ward system and regime, rushed and given an enema, shaved and then attached to a machine. The labour was a blur as the pain eventually kicked in. I was moved to a delivery suite with lots of medical staff surrounding me. They injected me in my leg, telling me "It's for your blood pressure". The nurse told me to "Push into you bottom like having a poo-poo" "OMG! What did she mean?" I thought, "A

Geraldine's Pearl by Marcia M

baby doesn't come out of your bottom". I pushed the best that I could and then they said "Your baby's head is here, it's here". I didn't believe them. I didn't know where Vince was, the room was dark and everything was blurred and I was high on pethidine.

When baby was finally born, he was dry and flaky and was whisked away from me. I was very ill apparently. I had pre-eclampsia and I had lost an excessive amount of blood. My baby boy, Solomon, was taken away to the nursery whilst I was treated, not much was explained to me but I was to learn later that I could have died from the condition that I had. I was moved to a side room and was alone for four days in hospital. It was confusing and I struggled with it all. The baby was not fed by my breast or a bottle for twenty-four hours; he had survived on water from a spoon; my son Solomon, 7lb's and 5oz's. I didn't know how to really care for him or whether I was supposed to change his nappy and bathe him or whether it was the Nurse's job, I simply didn't know and felt so bewildered.

Geraldine's Pearl by Marcia M

But I was not feeling right in many ways; the first two nights were dominated by worry and anxiety over what to do about my father. Did I want him to see the baby? Did I want to see my dad? I agonised over this for two whole nights and was wracked with fear and anxiety.

The trigger for this occurred about eight months previously when I had visited dad, as I always did as a dutiful daughter. I was eighteen and in the early stages of pregnancy. Suddenly, my father became angry and held me up by one arm and proceeded to beat me, he beat me on my behind, strung me up and beat me. As he was beating me he was cursing me for something - oh yes, apparently dad had a good reason for this unprovoked attack on me.

Ten years previously, if you recall, I shared about the night in Wales when I ran next door to get help? He was angry with me for doing that. Can you believe it? I was being punished for trying to save my mom? That day, as he beat me, I vowed that I never wanted to see him again and I didn't in fact see him for four years. Dad met Solomon when he was four years

Geraldine's Pearl by Marcia M

old, as in the meantime I had decided to just get on with my life, building a new future with my own family and I promised myself to make it perfect, much better than my childhood.

I was so vulnerable after I became a mom, I was still a teen, and I had been through a physically and medically traumatic birth with high anxiety over my father. This then brought about the 'baby blues'.

I changed significantly at the time. I hadn't realised it before but I was a bit of an 'IT' girl in my teens, well dressed, well-groomed, my hair was my pride and always on point. I had a Saturday job between the ages of fifteen and seventeen; I earned my own money and would spend it on clothes and shoes. So after becoming a mom I let myself go, they said, I focussed only on my child and being the best mother I could be. I realise now of course, that I was unknowingly in a type of depression. I had changed.

The flat that we lived in had mice and no hot water. Before we had the baby, we had replaced the coal fire with a gas one, thinking that we were improving the quality of our environment. However, we hadn't factored into our thinking that the coal fire was also the source of power to heat the hot water tank, so with it removed, we could get no hot water and no hot baths. It would take about thirty kettles to fill a bath and that was far too many to contemplate even after having the baby, so therefore I was unable to bathe. It wasn't an ideal situation at all. We also did not know how to budget at all so sometimes we ran out of food or nappies; those times proved to be a steep learning curve, becoming parents.

Solomon was a lovely boy who made me proud. Vince and I continued to build our lives together. He always worked and when Solomon was seven months old, I also went back to work. I found a job advertised at the job centre for a Receptionist based at the Afro-Caribbean Centre in Walsall. I remember that day vividly as they thought I was Indian and not African-Caribbean and I had to explain that my heritage was Jamaican.

Geraldine's Pearl by Marcia M

The interview for the Receptionist post went well but they didn't offer me that post, instead they offered me the Publicity Officer post which was full time with a higher profile and far greater responsibility. I must have impressed them but I declined the post as I wanted to work part-time whilst my baby was still young. My mother was a career woman; however, my mother-in-law was at home and gladly took care of her grandson.

To get to work I had to catch three buses, leaving my home at 6am to take the baby to my in-laws and then to proceed to work in time for a 9am start. It was heavy going each day, so I asked the Supervisor if I could start at a later time and take half an hour lunch to save me having to get up so early with the baby. My Supervisor retorted "We can't do that, that's why we try not to take on people with problems". I thought, this came from a woman and I couldn't believe it. So people with children were people with problems and again, my radar for injustice was bleeping, I knew that it wasn't right or fair treatment. I felt that my request was reasonable and

Geraldine's Pearl by Marcia M

legitimate, I wasn't asking for anything extra, just for some flexibility and understanding.

My only choice was to leave my baby with my in-laws for two nights every week so that I could work. Solomon was well looked after by his traditional Caribbean Grannie, who would saturate his hair with homemade coconut oil, he was truly loved by her and he responded well to her too. It was a good place to work and proved to be a great work experience. However, I was subjected to sexual harassment by an older male who worked there and used to talk to me at the reception daily. I was friendly and polite to him as I was to all others, but my friendliness was misinterpreted so much so that he followed me along the corridor and grabbed me to himself, pressing his large body against my slight frame and he kissed me full on my lips. I pushed him away and hurriedly walked down the corridor and found my friend, an older woman, and told her about what had happened.

I was a little shaken up but went back to the reception desk to continue my work. I was then shaken even more as he

Geraldine's Pearl by Marcia M

approached me again and I thought he was going to apologise but instead he whispered, "I've never tasted anything so bitter!" with such venom that it hurt me. So he really thought that I would like it? Unbelievable! I was totally shocked. That experience taught me to keep my reserve around me; I became aware that being friendly could be misinterpreted as flirtation so I drew into myself so as not to attract unwanted attention.

After having my baby my career blossomed and I again applied for a job as a Childcare Organiser with the Black Women's Co-operative Childminding Project. I was still only twenty and again at that interview they were so impressed that they offered me the Co-ordinator's position. I was terrified at the time as the budget was £30k, and I had never managed a budget before. I was frightened at the thought of so much responsibility so I took the Childcare Organiser's post instead still a supervisory role but second in command. The fabulous factor about that job was that I could bring Solomon to work with me and include him in the ratios in the Crèche that I had put together. We also moved home to a luxury apartment in a residential area in Walsall. The apartment had three bedrooms and a very large living room. It was carpeted throughout and was amazing. We had moved up and away from the mouse-infested place with no hot running water. We cherished our new home.

Geraldine's Pearl by Marcia M

Chapter Fourteen

My Journey of Choices

I was working with a group of the most progressive pioneering women of that time, I was so young and they were in their thirties and forties. They very kindly told me that I was a 'bright spark' and even though I hadn't realised just how outspoken and knowledgeable I was until I received some feedback, all that I knew came from my love of reading, that habit that my mother had instilled in me was paying off. Reading gave me immense information and that knowledge gave me empowerment especially as I was able to translate what I had read and learnt into valuable practices. Reading gave me the power to secure employment opportunities beyond my experiences and qualifications.

I embarked on a community activist path, campaigning for women's rights and most significantly for better children's day-care and we lobbied government about domestic abuse issues. I travelled around the country and Europe as part of a network of women. These pioneering women invested in me further through training and development, enabling me to gain public sector qualifications and they fully funded my driving lessons and driving test. They had vision and foresight and truly understood what investing in people really meant. This is the baseline for my whole career whereby I have invested immensely in the training and development of all staff teams that I have led and managed, it is just an integral belief and value and a way of paying forward the opportunities I was blessed with at the beginning of my career.

My career developed further just before and after the birth of our second child, a girl, Jasmine. It was during my pregnancy with Jasmine that I had turned twenty-one. I was finally and officially an adult! I had a twenty-first birthday party along with celebrating Solomon's second birthday. I went shopping with my mom for my party outfit as she was treating me and I found a super sexy gold dress that I wanted to wear as after all I was turning twenty-one! But mom discouraged me saying how my being pregnant meant that I needed something that

Geraldine's Pearl by Marcia M

would grow with the pregnancy, so she encouraged me to have a skirt and blouse that made me look ten years older and feeling like a frump. Nevertheless, I went along with mom's ideas. I was quite skinny in the early stages of my pregnancy and was not showing and although I didn't really agree with mom's logic, I had succumbed and agreed to her ideas again.

All that aside, the months of pregnancy were very difficult and our marriage was severely tested. Vince's behaviour had become erratic. He was always out and even though this was nothing new and he went out a lot to pubs, clubs, dances and blues parties, during those times it was extremely stressful; nothing that I said or did would encourage him to stay at home with me and Solomon. I would stand at the front door and cry and plead with him as I cried out "Please don't go out". I begged him "Don't leave us again".

I was lonely and isolated but he would simply brush past me and leave the home allowing nothing to stop him from doing what he had planned. This had been happening since I had left my parents' home to live with him three years earlier. It wasn't nice and I couldn't stop him so therefore I was distressed and desperately needed company. On one occasion I walked down to my parents' house with Solomon, feeling really upset and distressed. I needed my family but I did not receive the kindness that I was seeking as my stepfather told me quite bluntly that "You can't keep running back to us when you and your husband have had an argument!" I was hurt and astounded and I thought to myself, "Well if I cannot go to my parents when I was hurting, where could I go?" I was confused. I soon began to painfully learn that my family didn't have much understanding or empathy for me or my situation. I felt out-casted, like an outsider who belonged nowhere.

Nevertheless, I continued to thrive in the workplace, building my career and just as I had enjoyed school, I enjoyed my work and I was excelling. You see, achieving was my default, my distraction from pain, my place of belonging, my way of proving and approving of myself.

Geraldine's Pearl by Marcia M

I deliberately took better care of myself during that second pregnancy, I ate sensibly, no junk foods, more fruit and vegetables and I watched my weight. I didn't want to pile on the weight like I had in my first pregnancy. I also bought nice clothes, expensive maternity wear; I could afford to do this as I was in a well-paid job. When I was expecting Solomon, I had borrowed a lot of clothing all from older women, turning me into a young but older looking frump, I had lost my youth, I had lost myself, and I was like an old woman. "Not this time" I said resignedly to myself, "I'm young and I'm staying young".

With the ongoing marriage problems, I developed a crush on a co-worker, he was so friendly and kind to me at work and I also found him really attractive. Vince had been really messing me about, he even stayed out some nights during which I would stay awake worrying about him, it was a testing time as I stated earlier. Then one weekday, I just did not go home, I didn't want to. My feelings had developed and were really overwhelming. I sat in the office talking with my co-worker, the object of my infatuation, for hours and hours until it was really late and I still didn't want to go home. I didn't drive and had missed the last bus, so I went and spent the night with him. I had reached a point of no return with Vince or so I thought at the time.

We spent a beautiful, comforting and peaceful night together. Little did we know of the drama that my husband had created, the police had been called, and he kept swallowing down cans of Tennants Super beers. He and my parents and the police were looking for me. He was in such an inconsolable mental and emotional state. Yet he had never once thought of calling me those nights that he had stayed away from our home leaving me all alone. When I arrived home, he had proceeded to chase after me with a kitchen knife and I had to leap down a flight of stairs to get away from him. Even at five months pregnant I was a fast runner and very nimble so was able to get away from him.

I had simply had enough. I had felt that the marriage was over. Then a few months later, our beautiful daughter was born. It had been a very stressful birth and I was totally and shockingly unprepared for the pains. I hadn't attended ante-

Geraldine's Pearl by Marcia M

natal classes. I wanted pethidine injections but this was denied me. The hospital staff were sure that my labour would be short, not long enough to warrant the use of an opiate drug. It was only three hours in regards to my labour but I really panicked with the pain of it. I stood up on the bed, I couldn't control myself, and I was far less composed and not at all dignified. I heard the staff say "She's one of them". I mean it was so dangerous for a woman in advanced labour to be standing up on the bed, I mean what if I fell? I just can't imagine what I was thinking or not thinking, as the case may be.

When our baby girl Jasmine was born her eyes just 'sparkled'. I turned to Vince and gasped "Look at her eyes, look at her eyes". They were huge and beautiful, they sparkled, she was beautiful and only weighed 6lb and 14 ounces and smaller than my son had been. I thought babies were meant to get bigger each time but "Maybe it's because she's a girl".

We went back home and settled into life with our two children. Once again Vince's' behaviour was erratic and he had even made plans to leave me and go to the Carnival days after the birth whilst conveniently omitting to tell me this. One Sunday afternoon a group of our friends arrived whilst I was sat up in bed with the baby, just about to eat my dinner. I was excited as I thought they had come to visit us all but they hadn't: they were all on their way out and were just there picking Vince up. Well, I went crazy, throwing my dinner and the remote control against the wall. "How could they?!", "How could he?!" I raged in my mind.

My adulthood was teaching me to be a loner, to be independent and strong and how to cope with rejection.
A very painful learning experience of how this manifested was one New Year's Day when the children were one year and three years old and our car was off the road. My family had promised to come and collect us all so that we could all be a part of a family gathering at my aunt's house, this was an occasion for the whole of my mom's family. We got ready, the children, me and my husband, excited for the special gathering of families with loved ones. Our telephone only

received incoming calls as it was my way of maintaining financial control, and it had turned out to be a rainy day.

We waited and waited but nobody came, so Vince walked to the telephone box and called my aunt's house. They reassured him that someone was coming for us. I was relieved on hearing this and waited patiently. We waited another ninety minutes and still no-one came and no-one called. It was New Year's Day and I had no food prepared for us as we were going to the family get-together. So once again, Vince went to the telephone box in the heavy rain and called them again. They again said that they were coming. But nobody came. No mother, no stepfather, uncle or grandfather, no-one. Not one of them had felt that it was the right thing to collect me and my family. I was devastated and I internalised this experience and how I had felt rejected and unvalued along with my children. I couldn't believe that my family would do this to me and my children. It had been so heart-breaking for me and I couldn't tell you what we ate that day but I know that I cried myself to sleep.

It's an experience that I have never received an explanation or apologies for. I still do not understand other than it showed complete heartlessness and a lack of respect or kindness towards me and my family unit. We were excluded.

Yet again my inner strength, my resilience and my protective default modes of survival came to the fore. In my mind I had received confirmation that I could only rely on me.

I hadn't been equipped with such resilience for no reason. My motto even from those early days and times was "The greatest revenge is success" so I focussed on just that, creating a happy family unit, raising my children and doing well in my career and studies, focussing on being better. This approach soothed me and distracted me from my emotional distress many a time. Even as I write this book, I am aware that I am channelling my pains into completing this task, engrossing myself in my journey to success.

Geraldine's Pearl by Marcia M

Chapter Fifteen
Bouncing Back

Recently I have defined myself as the 'Bounce-Back-Ability Queen'. I bounce back from obstacles and adversities quickly; I keep going, forgive and move on. There are some circumstances that I just did not understand at the time that they happened and I still don't fully understand. However, rather than dwell on the issues and hold on to inner anger, upset and hurt, I would dig deeper inside myself and reach out to God who had always been my source of strength and comfort.

Life ticked away quite steadily and we were financially comfortable. At aged twenty, I became a Co-ordinator of a Voluntary Organisation and Vince held down a good job making UPVC windows. Vince's behaviour was sometimes erratic, he was a very exciting character anyway but strange things would happen, like money going missing from our bank account and him returning home with a gold bracelet or

Geraldine's Pearl by Marcia M

having his teeth filed down and replaced with gold ones. One time he had broken his leg, telling me that he had slipped on a kerb whilst out working but that was not true. I found out that he had broken it playing football. He hadn't been to work at all. The journey to the hospital involved him knocking back numerous cans of Tennants Super beers and smoking 'weed' to distract from the pain. This was the way that Vince always medicated himself, whether it was an emotional or physical pain, it hadn't mattered to him. There were so many incidents, too many to name, but things got so bad that we received complaints from our neighbours. In actual fact the neighbours had put together a petition to get us out and I hadn't understood why.

I was out at work every day but for eight weeks Vince was at home whilst his broken leg was healing, the children were at school and nursery. As it transpired, Vince had been having parties during the day time, blasting music, smoking weed and generally making a nuisance of himself every day of the week whilst I had been out of the house, working.

Geraldine's Pearl by Marcia M

I was so embarrassed, so ashamed – "What to do now?" I thought and had then set about getting a move as quickly as possible. We rented our beautiful home from a Housing Association; I was advised that the best route would be to advertise for an exchange. I put notices up in local shops and eventually someone responded and we exchanged our beautiful three-bedroom apartment in an exclusive area for a three-bedroom terraced house in an area much like a ghetto. I suppose that type of area matched my husband's behaviour.

We moved to the house and continued with our lives but the events that ensued were horrifying.

Geraldine's Pearl by Marcia M

Chapter Sixteen

Somebody Stop me!

There had been signs of Vince having mental health problems some eight years previously when at the age of nineteen, he went missing one summer after going to Notting Hill Carnival with his friends. These friends of his all came back that weekend but it took Vince two weeks to return. For some reason, whilst he was away, he had become psychotic. Some blamed it on the 'weed' and others said that he had taken cocaine and the majority of them just went around saying that he had gone 'MAD'.

At age sixteen I was smitten, we had been together for a year. I would sneak away from my home to visit him in All Saints Hospital, against my parents' instructions. Vince had been sectioned under the Mental Health Act. I didn't quite understand what had happened but I was in love with him, I saw beyond the present situation and loved him for who he was to me.

Geraldine's Pearl by Marcia M

Somehow we got through that episode and our relationship grew strong. We had married, had children and now lived in a three-bed terrace that we had been forced to exchange for. Vince's behaviour had seemed to have settled down and he had not been in hospital at all between the ages of nineteen and twenty-seven, a good eight years, excepting the broken leg episode.

When he was twenty-seven and I was twenty-four, I had to be the responsible one and he had continued to be so carefree. His behaviour became extreme and illogical and at this point I have to use the word 'manic' for this was the beginnings of his mental illness pertaining to Rapid Cyclical Bi-Polar Affective Mood Disorder. Vince would be high most of the time, not on drugs but due to his own chemicals within his brain. His neurotransmitters were firing on all cylinders. Then serious changes of mood and behaviour occurred, he began with taking excessive lengths of time off work for no reason or taking laxatives then calling in sick because he had diarrhoea. At night he wouldn't stay in bed, in fact many nights I would waken in the early hours to find his space in the bed empty.

Geraldine's Pearl by Marcia M

He had been like this at times since the beginning of our life together. One weekend, a Friday evening, he left to go to the shop for some pop and didn't return until the Sunday evening. I went through so much ongoing angst in those days, knowing that I may have had to get up and go to work and tend to the children as normal despite being worried sick about him and his whereabouts. At those times I experienced a range of emotions, of thoughts, of feelings, questions and worry. It was agonising. Vince always gave an implausible explanation which I accepted for the sake of peace. I forgave him and was just relieved that he was back and OK. I loved him and trusted him, he had a way of making me feel loved, special, and I was secure in the trust that I had for him and he for me.

This I did, time after time, for twelve years. There would be months that were so extremely stressful where I had to forget about being a part of a team and just take on all of the responsibilities to hold my family together. Then there would be months when I would fall back deeply in love with Vince, the times when he was his helpful, loving and supportive self. I would be ecstatically happy and feeling secure until he

Geraldine's Pearl by Marcia M

would spiral out of control again, going out all of the time, spending money, our money, on jewellery, clothing, gold teeth and 'weed' and on living up to his image of being a very flamboyant, trend-setting exhibitionist. I loved the way he dressed and his distinct style, he would experiment with having diamond patterns cut into his hair and his eyebrows, he would also try applying various colours to his hair. He loved designer clothing from socks to head gear. In those days, he wore 'Pringle' jumpers, silk shirts then moved on to 'Travel Fox' shoes and 'Tachinni' and "Adidas" track suits. He always wore fashions and trends before everyone else.

The summer of 1993 was crazy. We were being filmed for a television documentary about parenting, for Channel 4. We had the camera crew and researchers with us at home with our children, going about our daily lives and we were interviewed about parenting. It was really exciting and enriching; we and the children enjoyed the experience and were looking forward to meeting the rest of the featured families on a trip to a theme park later in the year. Then throughout one of the interview sessions, Vince sat there

Geraldine's Pearl by Marcia M

drinking Tennants Super beers again and falling asleep during the interview. This was weird. Around those times he had disappeared with the car routinely maybe for a few hours or a day or a number of days, who could guess: he had lost his job that he had held down for six years.

In the lead up to this episode, we had worked hard together to get him through an Access Course at College and he had successfully secured a place at University in Wrexham to Study a BA in Youth and Community Work. I was studying for a Social Sciences Degree, part time, with Coventry University and was managing a play centre in Heath Town Wolverhampton. Life got a whole lot more stressful and confusing, with routine disappearances and pacing about at night, playing dance/ rave music, dressing and undressing and obsessive spraying of Lynx Africa body spray, he would just stand and spray from the top of his head incessantly. This happened on a daily basis for weeks and the music, rave music, jungle music, the 'Rat Pack' 'let me be your fantasy' - the smells and sounds, are still a reminder, a trigger of the memories of that painful time even to this day, some twenty-

Geraldine's Pearl by Marcia M

three years later. Vince had embraced the 'rave' scene and had embarked on his lifetime habit of Class A drug-taking, unbeknownst to me. I know he came home spaced out and smelling differently, his breath smelt strange. I am a very sensory person and take note of smells and textures etc. This practice of his was that which triggered the Bi-polar Disorder. I recall him going out to a rave one night, dressed in his attire, jewellery chains, bracelets and rings, returning home at 7am or there about, smelling strange, naked with no jewellery.

I couldn't even conceptualise what had happened to him, it was totally beyond my frame of reference. My life was engrossed in being a mother and building my career. I didn't have a social life, I left that to him; well the true reality was that there was not space for me to have a social life or a big personality as there was just not enough room in the relationship for this so I left the 'fun' aspects of our life to Vince.

I had heard later from his 'friends/observers' that he went crazy, stripping off all of his clothes and running around the rave naked after taking some ecstasy. I know that he had lost his jewellery and became a real talking point to the people around him. I did not know what to do, I was confused. I didn't know he was taking drugs, I didn't know what was happening; did he have another woman and was our marriage at an end? What was going on? Things had escalated out of control.

I was bewildered, distraught and feeling very heart-broken. I had to maintain a routine for my children, make life consistently stable and nurturing for them. I couldn't believe that my life was becoming a nightmare, full of turmoil, confusion and chaotic changes. The 'fear feeling' from my childhood started to come back, all of my efforts to provide a stable, consistent, secure home for my children was being destroyed. I was being destabilised and derailed. I went to work in a state and spoke with my Line Manager about what was happening, she could see that I was at my wits end and she suggested that I took a good break from work perhaps taking the whole of the summer off: "You can't focus on work when your whole life is falling apart Marcia," she affirmed.

Geraldine's Pearl by Marcia M

That was it. My life was falling apart and it seemed to me that all that I had worked to build for myself and my children was disappearing: my desire to give them a childhood that I didn't have, one free from chaos, fear and drama. I had wanted them to feel safe and secure and just to simply focus on being children. I broke down in tears for my heart was truly breaking and I was also in shock and grieving for all that I had lost and was losing. I visited my Doctor the following day and I was signed off with 'general debility'. I had never heard that term before but it seemed to aptly describe my current affliction.

This did not hinder me from seeking help for him, getting him to the Doctor after a struggle, explaining his actions, allowing him to be observed to assess his condition. I also had to hire a car for me and the children to get around as he was still disappearing with our car. I would be informed with stories of his continuous escapades and sometimes he would be so animated and enigmatic and then at other times he would cry like a baby. Vince's crying is a common feature of his life to this day but back then it was surprising and it was just not understandable how he would bawl like a baby about losing a

Geraldine's Pearl by Marcia M

football match and then at other times exhibit traits of complete 'manic behaviours' and be animated rather like 'The Mask' – "Somebody stop me!" with a huge ear to ear grin.

Between me and my parents we managed to get him to the Doctors, the GP would see his agitation and his peculiar moods whilst assessing him and recommending voluntary admission to a psychiatric unit in a hospital near to Lichfield. It was evident that he was having a nervous breakdown. I had to telephone the TV film makers and halt the filming because of our circumstances and they swiftly removed us from the programme and promised to send us a copy of the filming that had taken place to date: this was never received but they did pay us £100 for our time. This really wasn't important in the scheme of things. I mean at times, Vince was psychotic and delusional, running into the house when the children were in bed; once shouting that there was a fire and rushing to Solomon to pull him out of bed whilst speaking in a slow, exaggerated Jamaican patois, "Weh di Bwoy Deh!" and lifting Solomon out of bed. I didn't know what was going on in his head but it was frightening. He would speak very slowly and then very fast and it was almost as though he could not see me as he just looked through me. He would complain of aches and pains in his body. I recall my stepfather and I taking him to the Accident and Emergency Department, struggling, because in his state we had to use many a negotiating skills to coax him into the car with us and a little brute force, it was stressful and pressurising. I had had to leave the children whenever and wherever to tend to his ever increasing episodes as he was a very seriously ill young man.

Vince was sectioned on multiple occasions. I would visit him in psychiatric hospitals daily, making the long distance trip to Burntwood, to be agonised at what I would behold. Often, he would be drugged up so much by the pharmaceutical drug chlorpromazine, a pharmaceutical straight-jacket, tongue hanging out, dribbling, unable to speak properly and with stiff limbs, walking around in a continuous circle. He was still my Vince, the father of my children, the love of my life, my husband. I would compose myself of the shock and sadness that I was feeling on first sight and simply hold him and kiss him; I would savour the feeling and smell of him in the hope that he could feel the love through the thick fog of medication and mental illness. I was only twenty-four years of age, yet my love for him was deep, deeper than a lover and a friend; I felt a caring and nurturing love for him as well as being in love with him. I had a duty to do my best for him. At the time I was studying Psychology as part of my BA in Social Sciences Degree so I was able to use the text books and read up on the behaviours he was presenting. His symptoms were the classic signs and appearances of what was the commonly termed 'Manic Depression Bi-polar Affective Mood Disorder'.

Yes, he was just like the leading character in the film 'The Mask'. The Actor, Jim Carey, played that role with a huge animated smile, eyes glinting and seeing through you, he couldn't be stopped when he was manic, he was driven by an inescapable force that propelled him into grandiosity whereby in his mind he was a superstar, a super stud, super sexy, garrulous and charismatic and to the little children in the area he was like the 'Pied Piper'.

Geraldine's Pearl by Marcia M

Vince had flirted with the beautiful Egyptian Psychiatrist who came to our home one evening to assess his mental health. She was obviously used to this type of thing happening, it probably helped with her diagnosis of her patients. For me it was uncomfortable although I was aware that this was partly due to his condition. He would flirt and charm women throughout this period, even my cousin and siblings, it was painful at times, even though I knew he was ill. I mean I am only human and stuff hurts although I had previously been unshakably secure in the relationship before this, I felt pangs of insecurity overwhelming me. For me and the children, life changed almost beyond recognition. The peaceful sanctuary that I had strived so very diligently to create for us was now in a state of dysfunction, albeit for a very valid reason.

My visit to the Psychiatrist at the hospital to confirm my husband's diagnosis was surreal; it was a large room, in an old building, with a desk and chairs in the middle of it. I believe Vince was on the ward when the diagnosis was explained to me; I attended the appointment alone, without mine or his parents. 'Manic Depression' - I knew word for word the description of the symptoms and their manifestations. I was able to knowledgably converse with the learned man about the condition, the medication and the prognosis. Yet again, my ability to read and absorb information and to translate it into real life came to the fore - (Thank you, mom).

The staff at the hospital described me as a 'brick', they commended me for my strength but alas it was a tough task. My heart was wrenched as I had to drive away from my husband, my protector and leave him at the 'mad house'. That summer was crazy. As soon as I had stepped into the house my telephone would ring: "Marce, I love you, I love you Marce, I want to come home" he would plead or "Cha, me a come home" and it came to pass that this alas was not just a threat but a forewarning. Somehow Vince had walked the eighteen miles to our house, about a three- hour journey on foot; he was determined to get home. The door knocked and he would shout "Marci, let me in!" I opened the door, it was my love, my husband, my one true love, but he was very psychotically ill and he needed to be treated in a medically professional environment, so in his and everyone else's best

Geraldine's Pearl by Marcia M

interests, I would call the hospital and look after him until an ambulance arrived to take him back to the unit. I was still so young with a little boy and girl to take care of, it took seven long weeks of craziness, of Vince absconding from the hospital, after which sometimes he would come home and on other occasions going elsewhere. It was a crazy time for us all but we thankfully had a wealth of support from my parents, my siblings, my best friend (and cousin) Liz, all of whom went through it all with me as well as Vince's treasured friend Douglas.

At times the children had to be taken off my hands so that we could manage Vince's manic episodes, other times friends would sleep over, trying to contain him or holding vigils awaiting his return from one of his hyper-manic fuelled escapades. It's strange, but I don't really recall his own family being involved.

It was so very difficult, the stigma and discrimination and the demonising of mental health issues locked his family into denial and caused me to question my decision, within the

Geraldine's Pearl by Marcia M

community, for seeking intervention to help him. My own extended family I believe were in shock or denial too, as they never really asked me about how things were; they would look at me pitifully as I was obviously fighting for survival.

The chatter in and amongst the community was rife. Everyone had a story to tell about his antics and they relished telling me every last detail, despite suspecting how some of the stories just broke my heart. The story tellers didn't stop for it was one tale after another really, drama upon drama, degrading and humiliating, which left me feeling so embarrassed and ashamed.

People also felt that they had the right to pass judgement about me and about our relationship, all of a sudden everyone had become a blooming Psychologist and Sociologist: it was insulting and deeply wounding. I hated it but I held my pain inside and refocussed on what I needed to do to get my family through the worse of it all. It was only he and I in the relationship, other people were outsiders and they did not know anything and it didn't directly affect them.

Geraldine's Pearl by Marcia M

This was about our life, Marcia, Vince, Solomon and Jasmine. My focus drew me to a) Getting Vince treated b) taking care of the children and c) taking care of me, but in hindsight I don't think I looked out for me at all as I just got on with it.

I had been with Vince since the age of fifteen and this was now nine years into the relationship. Only perhaps twelve months earlier I had told some one that I was completely happy with my life, my husband and that we loved each other. We had a son and daughter, good jobs, a home and solid plans for our future. We were gloriously happy. I didn't know that fate had another plan for us; some may say that I must have jinxed the marriage that day when I spoke of my happiness, who knows.

Chapter Seventeen

Shattered Dreams

I could no longer control my life to make it better than my childhood had been. I felt defeated. I shed many, many tears and my heart was wounded deeply as my dream, my life and my vision was being destroyed by the ravages of mental ill health, yet again! Vince, although not physically violent, became very aggressive and intimidating over irrational things; this scared me as I could not predict what was to happen next.

My day to day became another blur of drama upon drama. I recall walking in West Bromwich Town with my children and my sisters and having glanced over to the other side of the market, I saw my husband walking towards my direction with a Rasta woman. They both appeared drunk and as they got closer, not only could I see that they were walking side by side but they were HOLDING HANDS! **What the F**k!** I rarely swear but this was a swearing moment as a massive rage took

Geraldine's Pearl by Marcia M

over me. I couldn't believe what I was seeing! I ran up in front of him and with my two fists joined together, I jumped up and swung and knocked him to the ground. He landed on the floor, down but not out! The brute force came from the depths of me, it seems that the force of all of the suppressed anger and pain had swiftly manifested in a rage at seeing 'my' Vince, hand in hand with another woman.

There was so much pent up emotion from the pressure of trying to keep it together for the children that emotions were bound to eventually burst forth. Vince reacted angrily at first as he and the feisty woman proceeded to cuss me. I stood my ground and then he soon scurried away with the woman in tow.

I made my way back to my grandmother's house with the children, feeling shaken up, confused and distressed, and my mind in a muddle. This period of my life was filled with incidents that were very acute and intense. Nobody really understood, I didn't myself, everybody had an opinion on the matter but this was my life, mine and my children and my husband. It was we who suffered the grief and loss, it was our pain.

Eventually, he was treated with the appropriate medications and things started to settle down. After being sectioned a few more times throughout the summer and early autumn, thankfully by the end of October he was back at work. Vince was recovering at home and we spent a good few peaceful months trying to heal from the wounds and patch up the damage that had been caused during the prolonged Hypo-manic episodes and illness.

At this point I decided to change jobs, moving from running a Play Centre in Wolverhampton to 'Nechells' Birmingham at a Primary School. I was due to start in June, the day after Fathers' Day. On Fathers' Day, we had had a BBQ at my parents' home. We had been seated at the garden table on a gloriously hot Sunday afternoon when Vince had whispered to me, "Marce, I feel funny." He had felt that he was getting ill again; he felt it and recognised it. That was a positive improvement in that he had more of an insight into his illness.

Geraldine's Pearl by Marcia M

This was the beginning of rapid recurrence of his illness; it had lain dormant for eight years then came back with a vengeance, so once more we were poised for another crazy summer. I started my new job against this backdrop, if ever someone was set up to fail, I was at that precise time, and the pressures felt were immense. I would leave the house at 7am to go to work. I did split shifts running a Breakfast and After-School Club. It was awful as it meant that Vince was the children's main carer and now it appeared he was becoming ill again.

Vince's character during 'mania' was larger than life like 'Buddy Love' in the Eddy Murphy Movie 'The Klumps', Professor Klumps alter-ego. Very exaggerated, opinionated and over-charged with testosterone, cocky and so full of himself, arrogant, commanding, demanding and extremely attractive and alluring. Our sex life was also transformed with Vince's sexual patterns changing with him doing things very differently and it was exciting because he was still so attractive to me. Gosh, I loved him so much, everything about him, from his aroma to the glint in his eyes and the way

Geraldine's Pearl by Marcia M

he called my name "Marce". Every night that he was in hospital or away from me I would sleep in his worn tee-shirts just to inhale his scent, he was the sweetest smelling, cleanest man I had met and he was so full of swagger and so well dressed. I, in contrast, was drab, like an old woman. I didn't see me as a priority as my children and my husband and my job came first. It was my duty to love and care for my family and this continued to be my way of thinking.

Vince's illness made him not only attractive to me but to the local children, they had found a local hero, an adult who would play adventure games with them. Vince, or as they called him locally, 'Tiger', was like the Pied Piper and children would just follow him, lots of Pakistani children. They would knock our front door, not calling for our son who was aged seven but for his father. Vince and the children had broken into an unused shop and had put up signs which read 'Under New Management' and they set about setting up shop with no permission or goods to sell, it was just a sick game facilitated by an unwell mind. My husband often spent all day drinking with other women: he was exciting and enigmatic but

Geraldine's Pearl by Marcia M

then would go to extremes like lying down in the road or stopping buses and redirecting the bus route and they had no choice but to comply – trust me, *this really happened!*

One Sunday afternoon I was at home with the children and received a telephone call asking me to collect him from a woman's house. Apparently, they had been out drinking together all day and only when he became too hard to handle did they call me, to help them. I dropped the children off at my parents and collected him.

One early morning, our house was raided by police at 6am with a loud bang on the door. I opened it and the police rushed in. They searched every room in the house. We were shocked and the children were disturbed by these events. Apparently Vince was accused of armed robbery of a large amount of clothing so they arrested him and charged him with this offence. I tried to explain to them that he had mental health issues but this was ignored. Oh no! My worst nightmare was transpiring in front of me. How were we to resolve this one I asked myself as a deep sense of sadness engulfed me "When will this end?" I asked myself. Again, I had to spring into action despite my huge bewilderment, finding solicitors who specialised in representing people with mental health issues.

The story transpired that he had driven the car in front of a fashion shop in West Bromwich High Street's pedestrian area and had held his fingers up as though they were a real gun, terrifying the staff in the store; he was somehow able to walk out of the store with almost £2000 worth of clothing, mainly Jeanswear.

In his defence, after conducting a thorough forensic psychology assessment, for which I had to take him to the Reaside Clinic, they explained that no sane robber would leave the scene of the crime and then return a few minutes later to change the sizes. It just wasn't rational and consequently the case against him was thrown out of court due to his mental health diagnosis. The impact of living with and caring for someone with mental health issues are severe, so much so that I was appointed a Community Psychiatric

Geraldine's Pearl by Marcia M

Nurse (CPN) to see me and to counsel me every week in my home. We lived in a continuous state of emergency. As I write, I recall the effect of living with domestic violence as a child and now consider my young children and the effects on them of their father's mental illness. Only now can I see that my son, my eldest child, was affected in a major way, especially taking into account that up until the onset of his illness, our home life was relatively peaceful and fun loving and Vince had been an excellent daddy.

Poor Solomon. I could see the pain and loss and grief in his eyes at the age of eight, especially in his photographs. I feel that despite my awareness of the needs of children, I had overlooked the needs of my children for specific support. My son, I believe, has suffered with a related malaise, ever since then.

I can now forgive myself for this oversight as there was so much to organise and major decisions to be made to ensure that mine and especially the children's welfare was safe-guarded. I decided that we needed to separate after three years of full-on manic episode after episode. I felt that I needed a break; I needed to focus on myself and the children. Vince's mental ill health had affected my health too. I started to show signs of losing it myself too, presenting obsessive compulsions including another crush on a colleague which absolutely sent me crazy!

In my pain I believe I reverted to exhibiting deeper attractions to men who I thought may be better for me or who just maybe would offer an opportunity to live out my fantasies and take me away from the harsh realities and heavy weight of responsibilities on my shoulders. This resulted in me being diagnosed with stress and having to take months off from work and my studies. I was in such a state that I couldn't sleep, my mind raced all over the place and I was destructively obsessed with this man for a good few months.

Once I had pushed this compulsion to the limit and had had an encounter with the man, the obsession had ended. Later on in that same year I left my college course right at the end of the programme. I was studying for a Diploma in Nursery

Geraldine's Pearl by Marcia M

Nursing and had achieved 'Distinctions' throughout the course; however, I was too unsettled to complete the course and not surprisingly, I subsequently dropped out in the final weeks. I felt like a failure, how I who managed childcare services could fail the course and friends whom I had helped along the way had passed. I felt like rubbish, doomed, sad and confused. The dream of a perfect life I had tried to create was now non-existent and my mind was in turmoil.

I pushed for us to separate so that we could have some peace and that I could get myself together. I asked his family to take him, to help me; they didn't seem to understand my request with one of his sisters asking me "Do you love him, Marcia?" Did I love him? I had loved him from the depths of my soul, I had spent twelve years with him, I had nursed him, cared for him when his own parents and siblings wouldn't or couldn't. Did I love him!!!???? The audacity of the question! I could have slapped her in the face right there and then but I didn't. I reminded myself of my mantra, *"The greatest revenge is success, do not get bitter, get better"*.

Geraldine's Pearl by Marcia M

I came across the following poem and it struck me just how perfectly sadly it had been written. It was and is so eerily appropriate to this section of my story, so I choose to share it here:

I destroy homes, tear families apart. I take your children and that's just the start.
I'm more costly than diamonds, more costly than gold. The sorrow I bring is a sight to behold.
And if you need me, remember I'm easily found. I live all around you, in schools and in town.
I live with the rich, I live with the poor. I live down the street and maybe next door.
My power is awesome, try me, you'll see. But if you do, you may never break free.
Just try me once and I may let you go, but try me twice and I'll own your soul.
When I possess you, you'll steal and you'll lie. You'll do what you have to, just to stay high.
Crimes you'll commit for my narcotic charms will be worth the pleasure you'll feel in your arms.

Geraldine's Pearl by Marcia M

You'll lie to your mother and you'll steal from your dad. When you see their tears, you should feel sad.

But you'll forget your morals and how you were raised. I'll be your conscience, I'll teach you my ways.

I take kids from parents and parents from kids. I turn people from God and separate from friends.

I'll take everything from you, your looks and your pride. I'll be with you always, right by your side.

You'll give up everything, your family, your home, your friends, your money, then you'll be alone.

I'll take and I'll take till you have nothing more to give. When I'm finished with you you'll be lucky to live.

If you try me be warned, this is no game. If given the chance, I'll drive you insane.

I'll ravish your body and I'll control your mind. I'll own you completely; your soul will be mine.

The nightmares I'll give while lying in bed, the voices you'll hear from inside your head.

The sweats, the shakes, the visions you'll see. I want you to know these are all gifts from me.

Geraldine's Pearl by Marcia M

But then it's too late and you'll know in your heart that you are mine and we shall not part.

You'll regret that you tried me but they always do. But you came to me, not I to you.

You knew this would happen, many times you were told, but you challenged my power and chose to be bold.

You could have said no and just walked away. If you could live that day over, now what would you say?

I'll be your master and you will be my slave. I'll even go with you when you go to your grave.

Now that you have met me, what will you do? Will you try me or not? It's all up to you.

I can bring you more misery than words can tell. Come take my hand, let me lead you to hell.

Signed: DRUGS.

Chapter Eighteen

Homeless and Rescued

I focused on my children and tried building some stability for them. I had a close friend who supported me by taking me out to socialise and one night I met a man who took over my life at this particular juncture. I and my children were homeless, we had lost our home and Vince and I were separated.

My parents provided a place for my children to sleep and I was offered a place in a women's refuge where I could not take the children. When I was given the rules they just wouldn't have worked for me to organise the children so at times I slept on my parents' sofa or shared my sisters' beds. Many nights I stayed with Eric, the man that I had met. We literally lived together in his one room place and shared his single bed.

I was engulfed in a cloud of escapism. I let go of my responsibilities to a great extent. I was off sick from work again so I would spend time with my children and then drive back to Wolverhampton and this I did on a daily basis. Eric gave me refuge, he was an organised person and he organised my life. Despite me having run my home for nine years and being a Service Manager for a number of years, I had lost it.

Eric helped me with lots of practical things and he was an excellent lover. I had been with one man for so many years so I revelled in new experiences and we spent every day and every night together for several months. I welcomed his enthusiasm and was glad to let go a little and perhaps escape into a fantasy world. I partied hard and I was out almost every week day through that summer, clubs, pubs, dances: you name it and I was there, spending my money on clothes and hair styles and alcohol plus I was also a heavy smoker.

I actually felt young and free as in my late teens and early twenties I hadn't done these things. I wasn't working and had full time support for my children but this could not continue forever, I had to get back on my feet. The job that I left running a play centre in Wolverhampton had a vacancy for the same job that I had vacated and the post had been re-evaluated to a higher pay level of £18,000, when I had left the pay was approximately £13K so this was a huge and welcomed increase in pay for me. I was ecstatic and so was Eric. We had survived on very little money since we met and now we could be comfortable.

After eight months of this nomadic existence and relative freedom I was offered a house in a nice, neat cul-de-sac in West Bromwich. The house was beautiful, nicely decorated with three bedrooms and a reasonably sized garden. I was thrilled and I was getting my life back.

Chapter Nineteen

New Beginnings

So I and my children started a new life. We had a new car, new home and I had to start from scratch again buying all new furnishings as most of our belongings were lost in the chaos and the loss of our last home.

For the first time ever in my entire life I had my own bedroom. I mean a bedroom that was just for me. I had shared rooms and beds all of my life and now I had my personal haven. I spent my hard earned money on furnishing my home nicely to suit what I wanted without any influence from others and it was a marvellous feeling. Life in our new home was really good, we were comfortable and the children started to excel at school and in various clubs. I also set up a mobile crèche and consultancy business and gained a place at The University of Central England to qualify in social work. We also enjoyed holidays in the UK and to Disneyland and Jamaica.

Geraldine's Pearl by Marcia M

I was still with Eric and he did loads for me and he spent most of the week at home with me and the children. He cooked, cleaned, shopped and organised the home and I had never experienced this before; his Jamaican upbringing had him well trained to run a home, so I was able to chill and enjoy, it was different and I was enjoying it. I also started to get my groove back. I was still in love with Vince but was also falling in love with Eric and he was aware of this fact.

I later became aware that Eric was not everything he portrayed, the relationship was highly stressful, and he was a womaniser, a 'Gyalis'. He was an expert at preying on vulnerable women. When I had first met him he told me that he had one child and by the time I had a child with him, my beloved Gerry, she was child number seven with one of his other children being born just three months before our daughter. It was an experience that I never imagined and far beyond anything I had seen or heard of. It was tumultuous with so much 'woman drama' that at times it was unbelievable.

Geraldine's Pearl by Marcia M

Although I loved him, I tried to leave him so many times but he just wouldn't let me go he went to every extreme to make me stay with him.

I finally managed to end the relationship at the beginning of the year 2000. We didn't see one another for over eight months, this was the longest time ever since meeting him that I did not see him, even at times when we had said we were finished, he never ceased to visit me. We had some dramatic scenes at times with him blocking my car on my drive and even climbing into my house through a small kitchen window.

Looking back and telling the story now, I have to chuckle. At one point I had started a friendship with another man who happened to be younger than myself. One evening we were sitting in my lounge listening to music when we heard my front door knock and I thought to myself oh its Eric again, I will just ignore him as he always came knocking but would go away eventually. Then I heard knocking at my back door then the front door again. "This is strange" I thought "He's not going away as usual".

Geraldine's Pearl by Marcia M

Then suddenly there had been an almighty bang on my door, me and the guy looked at each other alarmed and ran up the stairs. I could see and hear the door being kicked in and being broken down and then he was inside the house. The guy I was with ran through my sleeping son's bedroom and I could see this guy on the ledge, contemplating whether or not to jump out of the window. In my panic I thought to myself "Why doesn't he just jump for God sake" and my instinct guided me to gently ease him out of the window. He landed with an almighty crash! Smashing my garden furniture as he landed this all happening in seconds but it seemed like slow motion.

Eric ran up the stairs shouting and asking where the man was as he could see his car was parked outside. Oops! I hadn't reckoned that they knew one another and that the young man and Eric had had problems with women in the past. Lol!

It's so funny now, looking back. On occasions Eric and I have laughed about it but it was terrifying, I was petrified and I had thought that I was going to be beaten up. That flight or fight

Geraldine's Pearl by Marcia M

adrenaline was pumping and as always I chose flight, running to my neighbours for help to get away from him. Little did I know that the two men were running around the streets one being chased by the other, but their feud really had nothing to do with me. I called the police to get a crime number for the incident and they laughed when I told the story.

So Eric and I split for eight months during which time I entered into a brief relationship with a long time school friend but this didn't last long, it just petered out, especially as Eric had come calling one night and seduced me. I had found him very difficult to resist, to be honest. You see it was very hard for me to resist this man, he was to me, at that time the sexiest man on earth, I often had coined him as the 'lust' of my life as he brought out a sexual freedom in me that had never happened before, he was an experienced and skilful lover taking me to places I had never been. With this man I lost my inhibitions, even the sound of his voice would arouse me and I finally became liberated, creative and free from my decision to protect myself with a level of prudishness.

Geraldine's Pearl by Marcia M

A few weeks later my car window had been smashed and I telephoned Eric for assistance, he was always my 'go to' person for help with anything practical, especially car related, he always knew a man who could. Thus he came to fix my car and 'fixed' me, so to speak, at the same time.

I rushed to the Family Planning Clinic a few days later to take the morning after pill as I didn't want to be pregnant by him, although deep inside I had a longing for another child. I had even stated it a number of times to my parents and friends, I even said that I would like to have a 'Love Child', don't ask me why, I just did that!

At the clinic I was given a routine pregnancy test before they could prescribe the after-sex contraception pill, just in case I was already pregnant. I took the test and the result was negative as I expected, so I collected the tablets and jumped into my car. As I was about to drive off my mobile telephone rang. It was the clinic. "Come back" they said "you haven't taken the tablet yet have you" "No" I replied, "Why?" "Come back in and we will explain." I went back into the clinic and they told me that they were about to throw my sample away but it had then changed to positive. "Oh my days, I was pregnant" - my eyes must have jumped out of my head, I was in so much of a shock!

I gave them back the tablets and walked away with a certificate of pregnancy. It was unbelievable, I was pregnant! I drove my car home steadily and sat down to try and take it all in. I then telephoned Eric. He was surprised but very excited but we couldn't believe it. We had been seeing one another for five years and now that we were finished completely I was expecting his baby, the last thing that I wanted or so I thought. But I realised that I had attracted this baby by my thoughts, words and actions, she was a very much wanted baby. I was thirty-three, a career woman with a Social Work Degree and a job that I loved. My children were aged fourteen and eleven and I was a free agent and now I faced going back to baby days again.

Geraldine's Pearl by Marcia M

Chapter Twenty

Barefoot and Pregnant

This pregnancy was so different to my other pregnancies. In the first instance I was single but more importantly I was dissed by the father. It was unbelievable; the man who would not leave me alone for over five years left me completely alone. I had been accustomed to my husband bringing me tea and ginger biscuits in the mornings, rubbing my back and my feet when they ached. My husband had also attended as many ante-natal appointments with me as possible around his work. For this pregnancy I had to do it alone and also to face my family, friends and employers and staff with the news of my impending addition to the family. I was teased quite a lot as I was evidently single, yet a baby was on the way. My grandmother looked at me and said "Well, if every day you go to the well for water one day the bucket bottom augh drop out!" her meaning that if you persist in doing something then there will ultimately be a consequence. Although I had been with Eric for all of that time, many of my family and friends did not know him, only my immediate family and closest friends. Although I was a proud, respectable woman who had held management positions and had a university education, I was reduced to nothing more than any other 'Gyal' that Eric had 'bred-up!',(Knocked-up.)

Through the pregnancy I was alone and he even cast aspersions as to who the father was. I saw him four times during those nine months and I was humiliated by him and his family, all of whom I had met previously. Yet they seemed to switch into 'Diss the baby mother mode' as soon as I was with child. I was shocked as there had been nothing that could have prepared me for the telephone being slammed down on me or not answered at all. I couldn't believe it; I began to sink to a very low place.

Further into the pregnancy I received a telephone call from another woman who was also pregnant by him. We arranged to meet outside the address where he lived as it was the only place that we both knew. As I pulled up outside I saw her and also his eldest child's mom whom I knew quite well, outside

Geraldine's Pearl by Marcia M

the flat. We all had sight of each other and agreed to talk in one of the cars; both of us who were expecting revealing our pregnancy to his long-suffering baby mom. In a flash, I saw him run up to the car with a machete, trying to open my side of the car. I was frightened and as you've guessed, my flight mode kicked in straight away. I grabbed my bag, pushed past him and ran. I ran really fast as I just had to get away, I didn't look behind me, I don't even think he followed me but my fear and instinct told me to run. I ran onto a bus just to get away from it all.

Apparently, his sister had called him when she had seen us all outside and was worried that we were causing trouble. We had not been doing any harm, just talking to one another. I felt that her decision to call him was ridiculous, heartless and very disrespectful of fellow women. Maybe we had given her the right to do so as we three were caught up in a situation that was neither respectful nor loving of ourselves but we didn't orchestrate it that way, we had been deceived by her brother.

Geraldine's Pearl by Marcia M

With everything that was now happening, I was once again catapulted into another painful and very steep life-learning curve. Most days I would come home from work and then get straight into bed, it was the only way that I could comfort myself. Throughout that time, I kept a journal of how I felt. I remember on one of the days that I wrote *"I feel so low that I know this is the worst that could happen to a woman and it was happening to me"*. I was in constant pain. I went through the motions with my children, washing clothes, shopping, getting them to where they needed to go, I tried to cook but kept on burning the food, I lost the ability to cook properly so we ate lots of freezer foods and takeaways.

My son was a teenager, finding his way in the world and my lovely daughter a pre-teen. My son was deeply hurt by the way I was treated by Eric, he knew it was not good enough, he was disappointed and my daughter was angry and so they should have been. He had been in their lives for six years by then and now that their mother was carrying his child he left her completely alone. It was bad, very embarrassing and it hurt so much.

Geraldine's Pearl by Marcia M

During the pregnancy, my grandfather died, it was the first close death that we as a family experienced. I was already in the depths of despair over my personal situation and I was alone and pregnant and didn't seem to have anyone, someone for myself to help to comfort me.

The aloneness was really evident to me at the funeral when all of the family were gathered around the coffin saying our final farewells. I turned to hold onto someone and almost in slow motion, I could see everyone hugging someone and there was absolutely no one there for me to hug, seek comfort from or to hold onto. I held myself together throughout the day, I did not cry, I dare not cry for fear that I would collapse in a heap. So I held it together as I successfully masked my grief and true feelings of loneliness and separateness.

The following day though, it all came flooding out as I was accused of upsetting my sister. There was I heavily pregnant and really in need but I was able to hold myself together but again, this show of inner strength seemed to have worked

Geraldine's Pearl by Marcia M

against me as no-one in my family could or would support me in my pain, no-one understood what I was going through.
I lashed out and got really, really angry, I almost exploded as they accused me of something I did not do, and this has been the story of my life, getting well and truly kicked when I am down, being totally and unfairly misunderstood. I jumped up and started kicking the furniture and shouting and I finally cried a river of tears with my head pounding. I wept and ran out of the house. My display of grief and injustice had been interpreted as aggression and as I write this, I observe that throughout my teens and adulthood, my family have apparently found me difficult to handle. I was always very tough and forceful, I was mindful to hold back a lot but yet I was deemed to be overpowering, to the point that my siblings and even my mother felt and expressed at times that they were afraid of me, they felt that they couldn't challenge me at all. The thought of this upset me and left me feeling isolated.

Often, the only person that could relate to me was my grandmother, as she too was a tough cookie and she seemed to understand my dilemma as it was hers too.

Geraldine's Pearl by Marcia M

I suppose this personality trait was what made me a leader, a supporter and a helper; I could be strong when others were weak, I could show compassion and empathy but I also longed to be understood, to be heard, to be cared for. At this stage in my life I had lost so much already and was having to deal with more humiliation. I felt as if I was being systematically broken down.

The only consistent support and comfort that I had felt had been my God, even though I was not practicing religion but I clung on to my faith in a higher power beyond all human nature, a supernatural power and love. I would cry out to God through my tears, my moans and my aches and I felt comforted and this allowed me to continue my journey with hope and with courage.

Geraldine's Pearl by Marcia M

Chapter Twenty-One

My Blessing

My beautiful baby girl, my Chinese looking baby, my tiger-lily, was born two months later; my sister was my birth partner. I was in hospital for four days being induced and had a really straight forward labour; I had really prepared for this baby and was fully in control of what was happening. I did telephone Eric who had been around over the few days that I was in the hospital. He would pass by on his way to a dance or maybe a woman's house, who knows.

However, he didn't make it to the delivery suite until just as she was born; he was beaten by Vince who managed to walk in simply by stating that he was my husband. When I saw him waltz in during the middle of my labour, I had cursed him and told him to leave. He said that he was worried about me; such was his love and care for me. I had known this of course but at that time I was giving birth to another man's baby so how could I have my ex, who actually was still my husband, in the

Geraldine's Pearl by Marcia M

birthing room? It was all so complicated it was crazy. I think the two men crossed paths in the corridors.

This was my life, well complicated. Eric arrived in the delivery suite with his friend and I felt like I was their surrogate as they cooed over the baby. I think he fell in love with her straightaway and took his responsibilities for our daughter seriously. He telephoned her daily, yes that's right, he telephoned the new baby, and he would come round to bathe her and change her nappy. It was during times like these that I felt able to forgive him for the hurt I had suffered during the pregnancy and gradually I also slowly forgot the physical pain.

After a couple of years, we became good friends. I didn't have a man in my life for many years so although we were never sexually involved with one another he was still the man in my life as the father of my youngest child. In fact, we worked hard to become a very strong team in terms of being parents for our daughter and now she is almost fifteen and he and I are still friends to this very day.

Geraldine's Pearl by Marcia M

I have somehow now been able to put aside the emotional and mental pains and focus on what was important with both of the men with whom I have children. I was adamant about my expectations from them and in the main, they responded positively with only a few glitches here and there.

Both men got to know one another and any early animosity dissipated for the sake of the children and because of our combined personal growths into maturity. They both knew that I was no longer interested in a relationship so there has never been any confusion, we were not the type of baby mother/fathers who continued to sleep together long after the love and commitment had gone, no I was not into that.

I was also quite deeply wounded by the happenings during the pregnancy, I really had learnt the hard way about becoming a real single parent and being alone at night with a new baby, but to be honest, I actually found it really easy, the baby was so calm and content. She also took to the breast immediately and my older children, especially Jasmine, just got stuck in with helping, in fact we used to fight over whose baby she was. Jasmine has played a vital role in the rearing of her baby sister. Solomon at the time of Gerry's birth was slightly detached as he was growing up and maybe growing away from me, he was a teenage boy finding his place in the world with a mother who was preoccupied by her new baby and a father who was still struggling to manage his own issues.

Geraldine's Pearl by Marcia M

Chapter Twenty-Two

My house, my Home, my Sanctuary.

"God is my refuge and my strength, an ever present help in times of trouble"

Purchasing a new home, rebuilding, moving forward with my children was both exciting and a blessing. After the break-up of my marriage and the humiliation of my pregnancy and continued difficulties with my ex-partner, I wasn't one to lie down and die "Oh no not I, I will survive!"

I was bouncing back in full force by moving out of the home that I had been so very thankful for to end my homelessness.

Geraldine's Pearl by Marcia M

That home was a wonderful place with beautiful neighbours that I didn't want to leave; we had a lifestyle of dropping in and out of each other's homes in the cosy neighbourly cul-de-sac. I didn't even desire to leave the area, but my inner drive could not help propelling me to accomplish my list of aims, goals and visions one of which was to buy my own home.

Geraldine's Pearl by Marcia M

I was assisted in purchasing my property by my Uncle who is specialised in conveyancing; I also qualified for a part payment of the deposit through a 'home buy' scheme. I had no savings and had accrued a few debts as there were times when I was so caught up in survival or escapism that I would either neglect or take risks with my credit. At that time I was earning approximately £27k per year, a decent enough income for 2004 as Chief Officer for an African Caribbean Charity, so could well afford to go ahead and buy a reasonably comfortable home for my family. I jumped the hurdles, completed the forms and applications and after a short period of time I found my house. I had looked at quite a few houses before I found the one; there was just something about the feeling of the house, the tranquillity, the ambience of peace that drew me in. Having said that, I only discovered the feeling after I had made an offer. I was compelled and internally guided to make an offer on this house before I had even viewed it. I was obedient to that inner voice that was directing me and I acted on that voice only. The property was a mere eight hundred yards, literally five minutes' walk from my current address and on viewing I was sold on it. I loved

Geraldine's Pearl by Marcia M

the greenery, the flowers and shrubs in the back garden, reminding me of mom and Mike's home and their beautifully manicured gardens. There was a sound of harmony coming from the water flowing through the water feature, this soothed me and I felt strongly that this was the place where I wanted and needed to be.

The week before moving out of our loved rented home, we were packed and ready to embark into our new life. On the Monday evening, I received a telephone call from my Bankers alerting me to the fact that although all necessary processes had been completed and I and my children were ready to go, I was told that I did not have a mortgage!!! Horror!!! No mortgage? How could this be? I spent days corresponding with my Uncle and with the bank: they had found an unpaid mobile telephone bill, I had completely forgotten about this, it was £300 and this stood between me and my future so I used my credit card and paid the bill immediately.

Geraldine's Pearl by Marcia M

I had to get faxes from the company to confirm that they had received the payment for a bill that was four years old. They did say that there were other reasons but I didn't understand them, "How could this be?" I had wracked my brain, "Oh my God", my heart was sinking, this was turning into a catastrophe, my family would be homeless if the house fell through as I had given up the rented property and had to be out on the Friday. I had a removal company scheduled and everything in place for the move: "Was I to cancel? What to do?"

I was perplexed. "My Solicitors were handling the situation, contracts had been exchanged so the transfer of funds for the purchase had to go through, surely" I thought. But not at this moment, my bank would not budge, they informed me. I became quiet and spoke with my God and pleaded for help. My knees, my whole body weak and my teeth gritted, I prayed: "Lord how am I to get through this situation, this circumstance?" A voice spoke to me and said "Let go Marcia, you are not in control".

Geraldine's Pearl by Marcia M

In fact, I was completely powerless, so I obeyed; I remained calm and cool and waited. I continued to prepare for the planned almost aborted move and waited as I faithfully held my peace, maintained my dignity and trusted in God.

There and then I decided to get baptised, spoke with my Pastor who guided me through scriptures and declarations of faith over the telephone and I was to join the planned Baptism on the Sunday evening. My decision was regardless of the outcome of the planned house move, I knew that I had to just depend on God, the Father, the Divine and the Universe completely; this gave me peace beyond all understanding. I became still, ceased worrying or fretting over what may happen, I let go and let God.

Miraculously, on the Thursday afternoon, the bank called and a new mortgage was put into place, it was then confirmed that we would move on Friday after all, thankfully I had not cancelled a thing. So we moved and I was baptised on the Sunday, fully dipped and anointed into the holy water. The sisters of the church questioned how could I be baptised as I was not qualified as I hadn't completed the New Believer Processes that the church had in place, but believe me, I had been through it in a close and personal way, my journey of faith is up close and personal, nothing less but a personal relationship.

Chapter Twenty-Three

Faith

Being a teenage boy in Birmingham was not easy in 2001/2. My son was drawn to what we call 'Road Life', a street gang; he had everything going for him academically and socially, yet he fell into a lifestyle of drugs and guns. I am stating it just as it was - one of the most distressing times of my life.

I had always loved the Lord but it took my son's circumstances when he was seventeen to really sharpen my relationship with my God. I went to my grandmother's church deliberately and with purpose of faith on his seventeenth birthday and lay at the altar; I was compelled to pray for his life, for his survival, for him to get his life on track and for God to help me with the situation.

I put my son before the altar, I knelt at that altar in intercession for my child and I put him before the Lord and prayed as I sincerely believed that God would help. God was my refuge and strength, I only had faith in him to see us through another mind-blowing and devastating episode of our lives.

It had taken some time for me to really understand what had happened to him but without going into too much detail: my son's closest friend at that time, was murdered outside of his home where he lived with his mother (God rest his soul). The young man in question used to come to my house often to meet with or to pick up my son. Just remembering how my son often visited that house and his friend, reminds me to this day that my son's life could have been taken as well as he was at the house most days and the very day before the shooting my child had been at the said location.

The horror of witnessing the murdered boy's mother's pain over the loss of her child, the physical and mental effects on her, the shock, the grief, it was too much to contain, for all of us.

Geraldine's Pearl by Marcia M

Realising that this could have happened to my child too, I knew I needed God; no one else could help or would help. I went from one agency to another asking for help but they failed me and my son. No help was given and there was no-one in the family able enough or interested enough to help me with my son.

You see, I was seen as a strong female power-house, my uncle once referred to me as his 'super hero' for the way that I had come through the trials of life, but I didn't want to be a hero, I wanted a normal quiet life. It seems that this wasn't to be my lot, the one thing that I had desired and strived for all of my life since I was a child, continuously slipped through my fingers in blow by blow onslaughts of destiny and misfortune.

Now moving forward, I have learnt that for me, it was not about making the external factors peaceful but to find total inner peace, thus learning that external circumstances just didn't matter. In my pursuit for inner peace, I had no choice but to faithfully and spiritually give him back to God, and by then he was not living with me as he was living all over the place, places that I did not even know about and he was only seventeen. I did not agree with his lifestyle choices and I applied 'tough love' by making him leave. I had my principles and I felt that I had to demonstrate to him that his lifestyle choices and what he was involved in was not acceptable to me. Whist I loved him so very dearly since that day that I gave birth to him, he was the apple of my eye, my second true love, my only and precious beautiful boy, I felt that I had to be hard in order for him to change.

I let him go physically but prayed for him day and night, incessantly. I lay myself prostate on the ground and cried and pleaded with God to "Please keep my precious son alive".

When he and his friends would leave my house I would talk with them about prayer, about Jesus and teach them to plead 'The blood of Jesus' if an enemy came to attack them, I believed in the power of the blood. I also prayed for his enemies and friends and for their parents, I prayed for the families in the community, I prayed that young men would begin to see the true value of life and value their lives and the lives of others.

The prayer that stands out most vividly to me was when I had to pray as I lay face down on my front room floor.

"Father, today, I give my son back to you, he is yours. Thank you for entrusting him to me and blessing me with him but he is your child. I hand everything in his life to you and if he is to die, I am trusting you with your will. I also trust you to take care of me if he is to die, to take care of my mind, body and soul".

This was the beginning of an almighty outpouring of the Holy Spirit upon me, I entered into a spiritual realm, and I was assured that God was real by the supernatural 'touch' that I experienced: Hallelujah! From that day to this, my son is now twenty-nine years of age, my heavenly father has kept my son alive, twelve years after I entrusted his life back to God.

Geraldine's Pearl by Marcia M

On each of his subsequent birthdays I have rejoiced in giving thanks and I continue to do so, for the kindness of the Almighty and the mercy bestowed upon mine and my son's life. Solomon often professed that he had faced many life-threatening dangers out there on the streets but he always felt that he had a Guardian Angel watching over him. I believe he did as he had a prayerful mother, grandmother and great-grandmother and the anointing and blessings of God placed upon and within him. He was covered by prayer, saturated and brimming over with it.

I thereafter began a deep and spiritual walk of life, no longer focused on earthly things but continually praising and worshiping God with everything that He had blessed me with. "I will bless the Lord at all times; His praises shall always be in my mouth."

Chapter Twenty-Four

Justice

Alongside the situation my son was in, I was taken to court by my daughter's school for her non-attendance: this was such a hurtful experience and I am angry with the education system about this.

My daughter, throughout her school life from Reception to Year 11 was a 100% attender, every year she was awarded for her attendance and she was an achiever, a popular pupil who represented the school at everything.

This part of the story is an example of how a system just turned against and without a doubt, spectacularly and completely failed my family. I had successfully gained a new job managing a Sure-Start Centre. This career move was epic at the time as it meant a pay increase from £28k to £36K.

I was still young at thirty-six and I had confidently declared out to God and the Universe that I required earnings of £1000 to match every year of my life and now this was being fulfilled. I was overjoyed and so thankful to God. My Pastor assured me that God was just positioning me where I should be and confirming who I am, but I was so thankful to God as one of my career ambitions was achieved. Not really because of the pay but because of the kudos and the recognition of my knowledge and ability in the Early Years and Education Sector as well as my leadership and management skills and experiences.

I began in this role in May 2005, my dream job, a perfect day as the sun was shining, and I had had my hair cut and bought new clothes to commence enthusiastically in this coveted role. Unbelievably but true to form, on my first day, I received a telephone call to the office from my daughter Jasmine's school, advising that her attendance had fallen really low. She was aged fifteen years and six months and nearing the end of Year 10. "Shit!" I thought, my first day in my new job. I felt pained and exasperated and doomed, this was just like the day when Vincent had become ill just as I had started a new job some eleven years previously. My worst nightmare was surely about to become reality: I really had to prove myself as it was a complex role managing a multi-professional team and a new team at that. It was so tough, so hard; I had to chastise myself to dig deep, really deep, to find resources of strength to bring me through. I was so overstretched at that point but nevertheless I continued to fight and pray.

By the September, Jasmine was disappearing from home, she completely changed from being my responsible and reliable girl and became reckless, drinking alcohol and smoking weed and she also kept getting into fights. Jasmine went through attacks and violations and abuse in many ways at that time and yet again, I sought help, firstly from the school and then other services including Social Services.

Geraldine's Pearl by Marcia M

The school did not help and despite me calling them and reporting that she was missing, they proceeded to follow their inflexible procedures by sending the Education Welfare Officer to my home to tell me that she was not at school. Of course I knew she was not at school, I had informed the school days earlier that she had gone missing. They insisted on being so ridiculous and procedure-led, I got angry with him on one occasion and asked "Why is welfare in your job title?" he looked at me confused "Where is the welfare, are you concerned about her welfare? Or just the school's performance ratings?" It really pissed me off; I was frustrated at the lack of support afforded to me and to my child, who was clearly suffering.

At times I would drive her to school and she would swiftly jump out of the car as I stopped at the traffic lights and run away. It was a nightmare, there was scenario upon scenario, incident upon incident and I was beginning to suffer with stress. I developed a condition called Chronic Hives Urticaria and Angioedema: this meant that whenever there was a dramatic incident such as having to restrain my daughter and chase around to find her, my body would react with swellings and sometimes I would wake with one of my eyes so swollen and unable to open and it would throb and again at times my lips would swell or my knee, for example. It was strange, painful and really quite difficult to explain; only strong anti-histamine medications could help this affliction but they left me feeling drowsy and very flat.

All of this was occurring whilst my little baby girl, aged three, was growing around and in an environment that was tense, stressful and drama-laden. This surely affected the quality of her formative years as so much was happening around her and there were times when it was difficult to pay her the full attention that she needed. It was almost as if history was repeating itself and my ultimate goals for a peaceful life were to remain unfulfilled. It was rough.

Geraldine's Pearl by Marcia M

For me I was carrying it all on top of holding down a Senior Management position. At work I tried my best to present myself as calm and in control as possible but at times they could see that I was visibly shaken. My staff took the pained look on my face as a personal affront to them and ultimately my relationships in the work place were affected, as was my performance.

Even as my character was being assassinated by Jasmine's school, my faith was growing strong and I continued to pray and fast routinely. I fought and got help for my daughter through the Child Psychology and the Drugs and Alcohol Counselling Services. Members of my family also pulled together to help me at times when she was really out of control. There were incidents when I had to lock her out or even physically throw her out of the front door; such was the behaviour that she was presenting. Her behaviour was terrible to the extreme and defiant but she was still my darling daughter whom I loved dearly.

Geraldine's Pearl by Marcia M

The school didn't assist or support whatsoever, this child who had been their super star pupil for four years. To them, she was of no value and not worthy of their attention or support now that she was in need of specialist care. It was fine when she was winning awards for and on behalf of the school and now they had swiftly and shamefully abandoned her for fear of their data and statistics being compromised or affected.

I persevered in order to further help my child and to fight the court case. I was earning a good salary that rendered me ineligible for Legal Aid but because it was classed as a Criminal Prosecution, my Solicitor had found a specific fund that paid my costs, thank God.

I will never forget the first day that I had arrived and appeared in Court. Upon my arrival they had brazenly automatically handed me a form to complete. I asked the Clerk "What is this for?" and the Clerk had replied "It's for you to fill in the details for how you are going to pay your fine" she said confidently. "So, they were sure that I would leave with a conviction plus a fine" I thought. £2,000 and a criminal record - that's what was at stake here. This would be my punishment for failing to ensure my child's attendance at school. I saw a number of mothers completing the forms but I fought against their unjustified procedures and premature beliefs to prove that I had not failed to ensure my child's attendance because I had done everything in my power to secure just that. I fought because my whole livelihood depended on it. I was a professional woman, a qualified Social Worker, managing a Sure Start Programme in a politically restricted Local Authority Senior Management post, which required a Criminal Records Bureau Declaration, in fact all posts that I have held, required a clean criminal records check. My life and career were now in jeopardy, a career that I had worked so hard to build over a span of nineteen years at that time.

Thankfully, two significant men in my life came to my aid, one being my Manager and the other my Pastor. They had both written supportive letters for me. The Psychologist and the G.P and the Alcohol Services had also provided reports explaining my child's condition. For the trial I was also blessed with a Black Christian Barrister, who actually attended my church on occasions. After a year of bawling, praying, battling to get my daughter through this episode, it was pressure and it was stressful. Imagine placing a family, a single mother, under so much stress instead of helping. I asked many agencies including the Education Welfare, to help me in this matter of the court appearances and charges against me. One individual had turned to me and said: "You are more qualified than I am to help your daughter, I can't help you". There had been that unspoken assumption that I, as a qualified Social Worker, should be able to fight this battle on my own without the assistance that I was undoubtedly entitled to receive. Their audacity plus their lack of understanding, respect or empathy, was so bad that I had cursed them: "You are good for nothing and you don't care!"

Life became a blur all over again and on the trial date I stood in the dock and was cross examined about my parenting duties or lack of, as they had alleged. It was a direct, no punches spared, character assassination by the Barrister who was there representing the Prosecution Team. I heard his words and they hurt but I had stood firm and held my ground with my head held high whilst gripping onto the wooden railings of the dock, to keep me standing and steady. I had replied to their questions, controlling my tears and anger and the deep hurt I felt to my sensibilities at such statements made, for example: "You were a mother who simply had given up on your child" or "You were a mother focussed on yourself and didn't care what had happened to your child".

Nothing could have been further from the truth of our family life reality. The Barrister had resembled a little 'Nazi-Hitler' and he had proceeded to execute his verbal attack against me with relish: you could see the glee in his eyes and demeanour. Fortunately, my Defence had been very strong: my Barrister was sharp and addressed all of the points that the Opposition had attempted to raise.

Geraldine's Pearl by Marcia M

In the public gallery were sat my family and some of the Staff from the school plus the incompetent EWO who had frequented my home the previous year. By the way, no-one from the school had given statements in my defence or any kind of references regarding my daughter's previously excellent attendance, character and/or achievements. They had cowardly closed ranks against me and my daughter, but my God had an entirely different plan and I was found not guilty. I was also awarded costs and damages. I had won the case! I didn't get a criminal record and didn't get a fine! I rejoiced in the fact that they had had to pay me and not I them. What a result! I thank God for the legal, mental, emotional and physical resources that he provided for me to overcome this travesty. My aversion towards injustice had served me well again, strengthened by my determination, faith, resilience, principles, values and belief in standing firm in my own truth. The Judge's summing up was fair and I am forever thankful for this mercy in witnessing justice being done.

Chapter Twenty-Five

Consequences

'Put a frog into a vessel filled with water and start heating the water. As the temperature of the water begins to rise, the frog adjusts its body temperature accordingly. The frog keeps adjusting its body temperature with the increasing temperature of the water. Just when the water is about to reach boiling point, the frog cannot adjust anymore. At this point the frog decides to jump out. The frog tries to jump but it is unable to do so because it has lost all its strength in adjusting with the rising water temperature. Very soon the frog dies. What killed the frog? Think about it! I know many of us will say the boiling water. But the truth about what killed the frog was its own inability to decide when to jump out.

Geraldine's Pearl by Marcia M

We all need to adjust with people & situations, but we need to be sure when we need to adjust & when we need to move on. There are times when we need to face the situation and take appropriate actions. If we allow people to exploit us physically, emotionally, financially, spiritually or mentally, they will continue to do so. Let us decide when to jump! Let's jump while we still have the strength to rise.'

God has never failed me yet. Whenever I am still and abide by his instructions I am enabled and empowered to be at peace even through the traumatic storms of life.

I have failed many times when I have listened to man alone instead of being still within myself whilst seeking a clear understanding of that inner voice of wisdom. This part of my story will enlighten you to the most devastating, debilitating and destructive time of my adult life, a time that confused me, my church, family and church leaders.

Geraldine's Pearl by Marcia M

This is where the strength of my will and my survival default kicked in, the vital method that I used to distract me before the real and painful experiences were allowed to take over and inevitably led to where I succumbed to what I call a 'spiritual deception' and tempted by mere flesh rather than to God blessed desires. When I use the term flesh, I mean the mind of man rather than true wisdom.

I was extremely lonely and so tired of going home to be by myself. Even though I had my little girl, my job, the status, my own home and a nice car, it just wasn't enough for me so that I could feel more content.

That year, my parents were deeply focussed on their mission to emigrate to Europe and my children were still going through their own personal and individual trials. I was fervently praying and fasting for each of my precious children.

Geraldine's Pearl by Marcia M

Vince had recently divorced me, an action which although we were separated and I had a baby by another man; the fact that he divorced me was very upsetting as divorce was never my intention, I believed that marriage is for life and should be entered into once.

In seeking elevation to a higher spiritual level, I sensed and felt that I had been filled with the 'holy ghost' as I often times found myself 'speaking in tongues' and had visions and prophecies. The power of the 'holy ghost' had me on my feet whenever I praised and worshipped my God and as I moved and I danced, I literally felt as if I was floating on a spiritual cloud.

I then had two vivid dreams or visions, of a man in the church. The first dream was of a crumpled piece of paper with his and my name on it and the other was of a vison of me carrying the man across my back, moving around in circles. In the vision I had wondered how I could move like this, carrying this large man who was approximately 6ft 4inches tall and well-built. Then, when I looked at the ceiling, I saw that it was in fact he who was moving us around and around with his hands upon the ceiling.

Thoughts of this man began to consistently occupy my mind. I had then shared my dreams with him and my spiritual mom, who promptly interpreted my dream to mean that we were going to get married. This was very surprising to both of us but just as the laws of attraction dictates, the seed of spoken thoughts was planted and we began to move towards developing a relationship with the end goal of considering marriage. We began by spending time in prayer. We were concerned for and praying for both mine and his children at that time. My daughter's personal circumstances were acute at that point in time, so lots of heart-felt prayers and fasts were for her. We were both deeply spiritual but gradually we decided to become a couple. We attended church events together and then started visiting each other's homes. Then one night, after several months of 'Christian purity', we had slept together. We did it! I was shocked because I had then been celibate for five years and had had no intention of sleeping with anyone. It was my belief that unmarried Christians didn't or shouldn't have sex. I was mortified, crushed and confused. How could I have done this, how could we, we were Christian people living a Christian life.

I went to my spiritual mom immediately and had also planned to see my Pastor, as I needed guidance. I didn't want anything to get in the way of my 'walk with Christ'. I was advised not to tell the Pastor and to put it behind me and so I took that advice. But that omission still did not ease the tumultuous thoughts that we had crossed a line of no return.

In my mind I processed the sexual encounter as confirmation that this man must therefore be destined to be my future husband, because how else would I have sinned like that, I reasoned. This was the beginning of a whole series of

Geraldine's Pearl by Marcia M

thoughts and actions entrenched in deception, confusion and an inner battle in terms of my spiritual and Christian beliefs.

I was thirty-eight and he was in his forties and I had felt that as Christians, we could build a happy and faith-filled life together. I believed that my household, my home, would have the 'spiritual covering' that it so needed and that we both would benefit from being in the lives of each other's children. I did not want to be alone so as always with any project that I had set my mind to achieving, I forged ahead to ensure that this harmonious marriage would happen. I was aware that he had not been working or in employment, so I had set about finding him a job, which I did successfully.

We also needed sufficient funds to pay for our engagement and wedding so we had agreed that I would apply for a loan to cover the costs and that if the loan application was successful, we would go ahead with the marriage. I borrowed £4k and we raised another £4,000, which meant the marriage was to go ahead. We also had agreed to jointly repay the loan, splitting it 50/50. I had trusted his word, his promise, so therefore I had had no concerns about the loan being in my name alone.

I am finding this chapter really difficult to write as each word written triggers another memory and other instances of recollections of this particular experience.

Whilst writing, I am aware of the fact that bringing back the past and memories of pain can be harmful. I suppose it's primarily all part of the difficult process of searching into the crevices of my mind for the information that has been secreted away in my unconscious thoughts in order for it not to hurt me all over again.

With my awareness of having to protect my thoughts and my peace of mind, I shall carefully extract snippets and examples regarding this part of my life. Should it prove to be too painful, I will instead describe the consequences and effects of

Geraldine's Pearl by Marcia M

the short but Tsunami-like interaction between myself and this person that I had committed my life, my home and my children to.

So we agreed that we were to be married in 2006, we had set the dates for both the engagement in July and for the wedding in the December of the same year. I know you are thinking that was quick, because it was, but that is how it happened.

I had hoped that we could have waited a couple of years but the man that I had now committed to had expressed an urgency to get wed swiftly, so therefore, with all good intentions, I had worked towards making it happen. The emotional, spiritual, financial and sexual abuse began there and then on the very night before the engagement. I had not slept what with preparing the meal for the family - curry goat, rice and peas, chicken, roast potatoes, a typical Sunday dinner, something that I was so used to doing as I loved cooking and entertaining.

Geraldine's Pearl by Marcia M

What had unsettled me was the way that he had cursed me one morning for calling him to discuss arrangements for the engagement party; he was vicious and venomous in his tone as though I was doing something to hurt him by consulting him on the plans. I was shaken up and distressed; I put down the phone and cried. This was a horrible experience, especially as we were planning a celebration, yet I had felt crushed and wounded.

My spirit was disturbed and I just could not sleep but I had gone so far with the planning that I had felt I had no choice but to keep going and to trust that our faith would bring us through. We had been and chosen the engagement ring and decided what we were to wear to church that day when our engagement was to be announced. The engagement took place and we had invited both mine and his family to dinner at my house. The meal was well received but I had felt ill as I was so exhausted having stayed awake all night, preparing and cooking the meal. This was the beginning of a relationship that lasted a mere twenty-four months in total, yet the long-term impact it left on my life resulted in a devastation of my confidence, my physical and mental health, my credit rating destroyed along with my clean driver's licence.

My skin changed dramatically, turning black in patches and my scalp was covered in dermatitis and stress related eczema. The high cortisol levels in my body caused arthritis pains, my hair went brittle and fell out, my weight sky rocketed by three stones and three dress sizes. I became a shadow of myself. The vile and tension-filled atmosphere in my home slowly became a discouragement for visitors and gradually my siblings stopped visiting also. I plunged into a dark and deep depression.

I was living with a narcissist who was an emotional abuser. Nothing that I could do was ever good enough and I quickly felt so very much broken down and emotionally battered. But, like my mom, I was a fighter. There was just that recognition of something inside me that had helped me to develop

Geraldine's Pearl by Marcia M

strategies to get through circumstances such as this. I became shaky and very nervous; I became reclusive and hid from family and friends. The only place I went was to work and I even had a lot of time off from there too. At the time I had been studying for my Masters' in Leadership qualification but was not allowed to read! I was not permitted to buy clothes! If I did purchase any items of clothing, I hid them in the car. They were only cheap clothes from 'Next' clearance sales, maybe £2 or £5 per item, but nevertheless, I had to hide them as the resentment that I would face if he knew, was beyond worthy of taking the risk of him finding out.

If I bought him anything, he didn't appreciate it or value it. I myself and anything that I did simply was just not good enough for him. His mentality was that women should buy him expensive gifts as to receive inexpensive gifts was offensive to him. He didn't seem to understand that he was the one who was sharing the home that I had singularly purchased, renovated and furnished myself. My home was my most non-human valuable asset and I was sharing that with him, in addition to bringing him into my children's home and lives.

I wouldn't and couldn't buy my children gifts either, bearing in mind I was now earning £40K plus, yet I had no money and began to live like a pauper. Being in the church meant that we had to tithe, within the marriage I had struggled with my tithing yet he would sometimes put all of his pay into the church collection as he knew that he could rely on me to financially support him.

The person I married would then belittle and humiliate me about my lack of faith for not paying the full tithe. The man did not even understand my career and the profile of my job. It was not a 9-5 role. I would have events and conferences to attend over days, weekends and in the evenings.

He would do everything in his power to prevent me from going; I was now letting people down, in a big way. We were

Geraldine's Pearl by Marcia M

'unequally yoked' in the broadest sense of the term, our education levels were in complete contrast, and he had an extensive criminal record and a history of violent crime, pimping and drug use. I also had earnings three times the total of his. I was a qualified Social Worker. His children were known to Social Services. The only thing we had in common was that our mothers had the same name and that we were both officially 'saved' within our church.

Despite the false interpretation and prophecy of our marriage, I do not believe the marriage was of God's will and I thank the Lord for setting me free after months of chaos and mentally and emotionally challenging stress and abuse.

I was left feeling really broken down and I turned to my church sisters for help and support.

"He's abusing me" I whispered: everyone could see the visible change in me, the once lively, social butterfly, bubbly, chatty and high spirited person that I once had been had turned into a subdued wreck. Yet they chose to ignore me and my desperate plight and instead I was scolded and berated for daring to say that I was being oppressed by my abusive husband: I was told "You must submit, submit to your husband!"

The discord, disharmony and disgrace continued into the day of our wedding. I was a genuine 'bridezilla' as I got ready and dressed for the wedding. My nerves were shot and I was a complete and utter wreck. I was consumed with a depth of panic in case I was late and was almost hyper-ventilating over his potential reaction if I was late arriving as I knew he would react badly.

Thinking of such a scenario, I imagined how I would then have to pay the ultimate price of his response by being on the receiving end of his verbal abuse or worse still, having to contend with him giving me the silent treatment. He had already shown me how adept he could be in using the silent

Geraldine's Pearl by Marcia M

treatment as one of his abusive tactics against me, just staring at me with no response and refusing to utter a single word.

In the mornings, I would have to tip-toe around the bedroom that once was my sanctuary, as I made my preparations of getting ready for work. I couldn't turn on the lights or use the hair straighteners and I was on edge all of the time.

I had to cook every day, huge meals, for a large man who loved cheese and chocolate. In seeking comfort, I began to eat as much as he was eating and so my weight escalated rather rapidly.

Being only five foot and two inches tall, I grew heavier with each passing day. Our honeymoon was a holiday from hell. There were nights that I either cried myself to sleep or even slept on the floor. This man had a knack of being loving and gracious and kind to everyone but me. He spoke of his generosity to other people all of the time whilst doing absolutely nothing for me. I had completed all of the planning for our wedding and been responsible for raising funds to pay for it, and the little money that he had managed to put forward, he had constantly complained about it.

I had thought that when he moved in with me that he would be happier as he used to complain about how he hated living at his mom's house. I knew that despite the pressures of life, that my home was a proper family home and that there was lots of love and joy to share from within my four walls.

We came back from the honeymoon and in my shame, I had pretended to everyone that we had had a great time.

Geraldine's Pearl by Marcia M

Chapter Twenty-Six

Determined to Overcome Marital Obstacles

Ironically, I had returned home with a good tan so I looked refreshed even though I was feeling really suppressed and extremely unhappy. I made up my mind that we had to make it work no matter what, but the obstacles were obviously huge.

Let me just try and touch on a few of those obstacles that seemed like impenetrable boulders of solid rock to overcome!

Finances - he had an illogical expectation that I would somehow support him financially and did not want to contribute to the running of the home at all. He also made it quite clear that he resented that I asked for any amount of house-keeping as he had grown accustomed to living off of his poor mom who was solely dependent on her small pension. He also did not pay anything towards the loan that I had taken out on our behalf in order to pay for the wedding. To this day, ten years later, I am still paying off that debt!

He did give me money but he would effectively eat half of it and borrow back the rest, plus the fact that he gave me a small contribution meant that I paid for everything, every convention or event that we attended including every special occasion which had to be paid for. I was living like a pauper now with no disposable income and I had married someone who wasn't ready to be a husband in terms of providing secure financial stability.

Sexually - because we had had sex before marriage, he apparently suffered with his own self-condemnation of this act so therefore he insisted on blaming me for that first encounter of 'indiscretion'. Ironically, since his baptism, he was the church brother who had fathered two children by two different women whilst I was the one who had remained celibate for almost five years, but this fact had no bearing on his irrational thinking.

Geraldine's Pearl by Marcia M

There were times when I was unable to sleep with him due to irregular menstrual bleeding but that did not prevent him from checking my underwear, either for evidence that I was bleeding or that I was cheating on him. When asked what evidence he was ridiculously searching for, he suggested that it was inconclusive. What a violation!

At other times when I wanted or needed affection or to make love, he would exert his 'power' and say no, simply because he liked to do this. There were many nights he would lock himself in the conservatory whilst I slept upstairs. I discovered much later on that he was, in fact, on the computer, watching porn and then he would spend an hour in the shower, God forbid what he was doing in there.

Inappropriate Tendencies - the other factors that I consider as relevant confirmation that I had made the correct decision to end the marriage, were little things such as how he would iron my teenage daughter's clubbing or party clothes and assist her to get ready to go out. He bought her high-heeled sandals and a hand-bag. One time he had neatly folded up her washing which he had taken out of the dryer, including her under-wear. I came home to find her knickers and bras meticulously folded on her bed and I knew that I hadn't done that and neither had she.

Spiritually – he would pray with everybody except me, his wife. I would ask him to pray with me and his response would be: "Pray for yourself," yet he and I would kneel and pray for his family, even for his children's mothers together, but he would not pray for me. He also used the word of God as his weapons against me either by texting or verbally quoting from the scripture: 'A wise woman builds a house but a fool tears it down with her own hands' therefore calling me a fool because I protested or 'Likewise, ye wives, [be] in subjection to your own husbands' His meaning that I accept the treatment that he dealt. Other examples misused were: 'Not a woman to teach, nor to usurp authority over the man, but to be in silence', 'Wives, submit yourselves'. There were many instances of when I asked him to pray with me and he would tell me to "Go to hell!"

Emotionally – I was told on an almost daily basis, "Marcia, you don't love anyone but yourself." He would dictate to me and add "I don't respect you, I don't respect any woman!"

He would also strike up friendships with other women, giving them attention and appreciation, instead of towards me, his wife. One day, he dropped out of a family occasion so that he could make some CD's for a woman he had met at work; he even gave his jewellery away to some Australian students at the university where he worked. On mother's day, he left my house with flowers and gifts for his children's moms and his mom, with no flowers or acknowledgment of me, his wife, regardless of the fact that we did not have children together.

On our wedding night, he sat on the bed and had a text conversation with his baby mom as well as sending valentine messages to her when we were married. If I dared to complain about these things he would pack up his things and leave, taking everything with him, sometimes even down to extension leads that were being used in the house. He didn't care. He didn't respect me or my family, yet we continued to accommodate him and his family.

I would drive to Huddersfield to collect his sons and take care of them at my home. I loved them but he would persist and say, "Marcia, you don't do anything for me or any one." During one of these journeys he cursed me the whole one hundred miles. I was driving but he somehow felt compelled to tell me how awful I was and how I did nothing to help him. I was driving to collect his children to stay over at my house yet I had cried the whole way there, I was in so much emotional and mental pain. When we arrived at the house to collect the boys, they could see that I was in bits, weak, weakened by the continuous barrage of animosity.

Geraldine's Pearl by Marcia M

This man would side with any and every one against me as he tried to set my children against me whenever anything went wrong, telling them "It's your mom's fault, she caused it."

He was also very insecure within himself. He was the lightest-skinned of his family, very light to the point of being almost white. His family were dark-skinned and he had a vast complex about this familial difference plus he was tall and gangly and he stood out. The fact is that he dressed very gaudily! Tasteless and tackily dressed, so he stood out even more.

He expressed his jealousy of me. He described me as a social butterfly, telling me I was beautiful and the best thing that had ever happened to him. He was appreciative of me on rare occasions, but in hindsight, this was probably a manipulative move on his part to keep me in line and to assist me with having to cope with and accept his unacceptable behaviour.

Geraldine's Pearl by Marcia M

He staged dramatic protests such as stamping his feet on every step going up the stairs or sleeping on the floor in the living room, meaning that my children couldn't go in there in the mornings; this both disrupted and disturbed the routine and ambience of the household.

He did show some kindness to my son and my daughters, he was careful to do that, but to me? No chance. His 'protests' were because I had probably used bread from the freezer for his sandwiches, I had taken Gerry out for the day or I had looked at the preacher too much during church service or that I had bought something for myself or my children or any other thing that he had deemed demeaning to him but was in truth, rather irrational to all others.

Please do not be misled for I am not an easy 'victim' and I can hold my own. I didn't take this all without a fight. Yes, I did tell him about himself, I did protest, but this did not stop his hurtful and belittling words and deeds from penetrating and

Geraldine's Pearl by Marcia M

infiltrating my mind and spirit. After eighteen months of hell, he finally left me for the eighth time, which included leaving me in Europe from a family holiday to my parents, after taking every penny I had to pay for his emergency flight as he did not feel comfortable!

I had prayed: "Lord, if he leaves again, let it be the last and final time." Well, God answered my prayers and he had pushed the keys through the letter-box on leaving. I came home and saw this and breathed a huge sigh of relief. I had stood frozen for a moment; this was my chance for escape, for freedom! I was filled with emotions of joy, relief and gratitude as my eyes watered, my stomach fluttered. This was it, I was going to be free, and I was sure. I had prayed the prayer and God had answered!

I had called him and said "Thank you for leaving the keys. I don't want you to come back because you are not welcome, it's over! Please arrange for someone to collect your things, but YOU cannot return."

I think he was stunned but probably thought that I was bullshitting but the thing is, I only say what I mean, whether I'm angry or not, because what I say I mean, in that moment. I meant it. I had resigned myself to the fact that it was not ever working, that we were not representing a good example to our children or to our community and we were hurting ourselves and each other.

I reflect that we both could not cope with the demands of our married life and alongside our personal needs for healing and growth, we were not ready and it had to end! I am choosing not to go into too much detail as I do not want to appear unforgiving. Whilst I do forgive this man that I had married and also his family, I totally declare that the treatment of me was wrong, but I was made strong.

Geraldine's Pearl by Marcia M

Step by step, I rebuilt my life and it took me five years, five years of separation as he refused to divorce me and would call me every few months with ridiculous half-hearted attempts to reconcile and to also further insult me. These conversations just convinced me NOT to go back.

I rode out those five years of separation, not knowing when I would be released and not knowing whether he would want to claim mine and my children's inheritance and assets. I survived the burdens of public and church humiliation.

I overcame the questioning, the blaming and the false accusations, even the ridiculous story that his mother and sisters had fabricated about me having a double life regarding having a man in London that I had been seeing all the way through the marriage. It seemed they could not understand that I did not leave their son/brother for another man, they could not see how he just was not good enough for me, they could not see or comprehend that I had left him for someone else - yes, I had left him for ME! It was vital to do so in order for me to love me, so that I could have life, so that I could be all that I should and deserved to be.

This was the beginnings of my road to healing, the path to positively creating Marcia M., 'The Success Maker'. A metaphor that I used for this new version of myself is again from a TV series called 'The Six Million Dollar Man.' At the beginning of this programme the trailer says, 'We can rebuild him, we have the technology.' Steve Austin, the character, had been seriously injured in a near fatal car accident, physicians, surgeons and engineers worked together to rebuild him using the latest technology at the time and when they had finished with his broken body, he was six million times better than before, in every way.

This was from where I myself was re-made from scratch, creating a 'six million dollar Marcia', a different creature, with Love, Power and a Sound Mind, a fearless woman. A woman, whose life had sunk to the deepest depths and was now soaring to the greatest heights, embracing all that was life itself.

"When aspects of your life are exposed to public humiliation and character assassination and to the questioning and examination of others, outsiders, feel no shame!

When you know that everything you did was with a good and proper intention, do not condemn yourself".

Marcia M

Geraldine's Pearl by Marcia M

Chapter Twenty-Seven

Pearl of Great Price: I am Geraldine's Pearl

Grandma! Oh Grandma!

My grandma and I had a special relationship, I was her special first grandchild and I was known to everyone as her first grandchild. Many did not know my first name but I was known as 'Miss Gee's granddaughter' or 'Mother G's Granddaughter.' I spent my early years with her and she had provided the family safety and security that I needed growing up.

My grandma was very proud of me; she was my biggest critic, my confidante and my ally. We shared our stories and highlights and pains in our private conversations. Our relationship grew particularly close when I was approximately twenty-eight years of age, right up until she died and beyond.

Geraldine's Pearl by Marcia M

To symbolise our close friendship and relationship, on my birthday celebrating thirty years of age, grandma sent me a 'To my Friend' birthday card. We did so much together, especially shopping. I would transport Grandma wherever she needed to go and as the years passed by, particularly after grandad had died, we had grown closer and closer.

My children were blessed to have a great grandmother as part of their week to week experiences, we visited and socialised with grandma regularly and routinely. She was the centre of our lives. When we suffered the separation and emotional grief of mom moving abroad, for me, grandma stood firm in that gap and our bond grew stronger.

Throughout all these episodes that I have described in previous chapters, grandma would advise me, "Fear not Marcia, just trust in Jesus."

Geraldine's Pearl by Marcia M

One of the reassuring phrases that she comforted me with was, "You are a pearl of great price, Marcia." My Grandma adored me and I her. She told me: "Marcia, sometimes I'm down but then I look at your beautiful face and it makes me happy." I understand this as I feel this when I look at my own grandchildren.

The day of her passing, would you believe, as was the story of my life, occurred in the second week of me starting a new post as a Manager of a cluster of two 'Sure Start' programmes? Our family had been informed that she had days to live. Yes, it had happened again! I was in a position where I had to prove myself yet had shockingly and simultaneously received that most devastating news. I was in conflict, my career was very important to me but my grandma was my everything, the mainstay of my life.

Geraldine's Pearl by Marcia M

Psychologically, I reverted into emotional and mental denial, not wanting to accept this piece of news. During this period, I had observed as my family members and church members gathered at Grandma's bedside. I was also there, but watching them and thinking to myself "Why are they behaving like this, so solemn?" I was aware of the look of impending doom on their faces.

Wow! I'm finding this uncomfortable to write as I feel so much pain. I am searching for the words to describe those precious moments leading to her passing. In searching, I am opening myself to exploring those moments and the associated grief once again.

Geraldine's Pearl by Marcia M

Historically, Grandma had been ill before and had always bounced back to relatively good health. "She is not dying" I often told myself. "She will be better soon." I had hoped and prayed. My mind, terrified of feeling the grief, went into denial. I had convinced myself that everything that happened in that week was not real. The decision to deny was not conscious, it just happened.

I truly didn't believe that she was going to die.

Grandma was lying on her bed silent; she must have been weak as she just lay there. I stood to one side and silently and solemnly observed the actions of the people in the room. It was similar to the anxious awaiting of an impending hurricane, a loss that we imagined would turn the sky black, that would shatter us and leave us paralysed and fractured for many years to come.

Geraldine's Pearl by Marcia M

I had thought that I had been prepared for losing my grandma after going through the emotional trauma of our mother and stepfather emigrating five years previous. Mom moving so far away from us was very painful, there was a tearing, wrenching and aching experienced by us all. For me it was the actual loss of someone above me in the family structure. Although they were still alive, they were now deceased, disengaged, simply missing from our day to day and week to week life experiences. Our lifestyles were intertwined and we are a close-knit family. I lived just a couple of minutes away from my parents' home, so on route to and from anywhere, we could call in, grab a bite to eat or a drink and touch base with mom and with Mike. Whilst rationally we understood why they were going and fully supported this, emotionally it was painful for us, their children and for their grandchildren. We had a huge void to fill, they were the centre of our family, and their home was our home. The house had been sold but we would drive by it on occasion and focus on all of the good times that we had shared at Dagger Lane.

Geraldine's Pearl by Marcia M

When grandma's health worsened, I was so very conscious that my mother hadn't seen her in months as mom lived abroad, but was in daily contact by telephone. I had travelled to Europe to visit my mother a month before and had explained Grandma's condition to her, even sharing a video recording of grandma from my mobile phone, I emphatically didn't want my mother to miss the chance to say goodbye. My mom, due to her own health condition and related medical appointments, could not come back to England immediately. I believe that she was also weighing up when was the best time to come.

During my grandma's final week on earth, I had pleaded with mom to come over, becoming quite frustrated with her on the telephone one day as I sat at grandma's bedside, urging and willing her to come over, we needed her.

Geraldine's Pearl by Marcia M

The message got through and mom realised that this was the time to come and swiftly booked her flight. My own grandchild, Liam, had been born and mom had not seen him yet either so this would be the opportunity to have five generations together at one time.

Now, as I have explained, grandma lay there in her bed as we sang hymns and read the bible to her, both for her and for our own comfort.

On one really hot day, I was wearing a low-cut vest top and had to lean across her bed to give her a sip of ginger beer and on doing that, the whole room was astonished as she scolded me in saying "A you titty dem you a give me!" in her usual firm tone and then she lay back down.

I looked at her and giggled and said "No grandma, here is your drink!" Now where did that strength come from? She must have been laying there watching us and getting frustrated as she sometimes did and somehow with her strong will and determination, she had mustered up some strength to scold her grandchild – to me, it was a wonderful moment. Even more wonderful was that on my mother's arrival, grandma had sat up and lifted her arms to embrace my mom and cried out "Olive, oh Olive". Finally, mom had arrived. Grandma's decline was swift from that moment on and she only lived for just one more full day and it was evident that she had waited for her precious child to arrive to say farewell. Grandma had not eaten properly for three years, passing at age eighty-eight; she had survived on ginger beer, coffee and Jaffa cakes. She had always been a fickle and fussy eater and she rarely ate from anybody, so living in the nursing home she had refused the food and asked for her coffee in her own china tea cup, using her own evaporated milk and a spoon of sugar. She was diabetic yet she had survived for a long time on this 'diet'.

Geraldine's Pearl by Marcia M

The day of her passing, moving on to be with her Jesus, came. We had all received a call to tell us there was nothing that could be done for her except to make her as comfortable as possible. We as a family, her children, grandchildren and great grandchildren, gathered for the day, popping in and out, along with church family and friends. Her beloved sister, who was ninety years of age, made the journey along with our cousins to spend the final hours with Gee.

The vigil lasted all day. I had arrived at about 9.30am and we were there to sing, pray and comfort, and to receive a trail of visitors coming to wish her a safe passage. At about 4.30 pm I was feeling tired and we were all hungry. I had then left with my daughter to go to her flat just to lie down and rest for a little while as tiredness was overwhelming me.

Geraldine's Pearl by Marcia M

As I put my head down on the pillow, my mobile telephone rang and it was a cousin telling us to come back. We made haste and got back to the room. "She is taking her last breaths", someone whispered. My son, cousin and sister were not back yet but grandma waited, her nursing home room filled with already grieving family members, about forty of us.

We sent the younger children out into the communal lounge as we felt that it would be best for them. I made my way to my grandmother's side and stood by her head and placed my cheek to her cheek. This was my grandma and my best friend. We could hear and observe the shallow breaths, prolonged and heavy, her feet and hands were almost cold, then against my cheek she breathed her very last breath and she was gone! My mom said "She's gone" and I and some of those present, didn't believe it.

Geraldine's Pearl by Marcia M

My instinctive thoughts of denial were surfacing again. I walked around asking everyone "Is this real?" and heard their replies of "Yes" but I just didn't get it. I knew what I had witnessed however, my mind wouldn't accept it. I forced myself to stay in the room when everyone was asked to leave for the staff to wash and prepare her body but I had to stay to see if it really was real! Along with my eldest daughter Jasmine, we tenderly washed and dressed grandma with the help of the staff and prepared her to be viewed. Jasmine neatly tidied grandma's hair in her favourite style, parted in the middle with two long silver haired plaits at each side of her face.

Even beyond that, after the whole family including the children and other visitors paid their respects, I hung around in the room still trying to believe that it was not real or to seek confirmation the she really was dead. When the funeral directors arrived to collect her body, I stayed to witness her being placed into the body bag; I had to do it, I had to for my sanity, just so I knew it was real, and then they took her away.

Geraldine's Pearl by Marcia M

Nothing could have prepared me for the pain of this loss, the physical pain was all consuming, almost too much to bear, my body literally hurt all over. I drank copious amounts of alcohol to help me sleep. In the morning, the pain gripped me in my bed, I could not function, I could not dress or eat or speak, and I was suffering a pain that I could not control and that which painkillers could not relieve. The grief over my mother moving away became insignificant against the intensity of this feeling. This pain was almost too much to bear.

We worked together as a team organising and planning my grandmother's funeral. We did not have to do too much as she had written her funeral plans in a letter to us all, scheduled to be read after her death. Grandma had planned every scripture, every song and tribute that she wanted, she had also named each person that was to read the scriptures. In her letter, she told us to be brave and that she was now resting with the Lord!

Geraldine's Pearl by Marcia M

Grandma had allocated my children their roles and to me she had given the responsibility of delivering her final message to the world, an honour that even in the depths of my grief, I cherished dearly.

Geraldine's Pearl by Marcia M

"This is my word to everyone. My life was fully spent serving the Lord. There is no better way, I love the Lord, and I love to be in church with the people of God. I was never weary serving the Lord, it's a beautiful thing to know you have hope, our hope is in the Lord and no one else, for if in this life we did not have hope we would be like men most miserable. Thank God I know Jesus and I will be with him throughout the countless ages of eternity, praise God. Loved ones, who are not saved, get right with God and find peace in your soul.

God richly bless you all. Time is short. Now is the time to accept the Lord. Tomorrow may be too late. God loves you.

Good Night.

(Geraldine)

Geraldine's Pearl by Marcia M

Wow! Okay, so my grandmother had made a conscious decision to write this message to the congregation. The depth of thinking, planning and leadership responsibilities was evident in her actions, also her selflessness in having shared her good news story.

Grandma's final message tells of faith and hope and surely it reminds us that we must have faith in something higher than ourselves to find peace, as peace comes from a place far beyond our jurisdiction. Grandma was committed to exalt her Saviour and to touch lives even in her death. This was truly and powerfully evident in the way that I also stumbled upon a familiar phrase whilst searching the bible in preparation for her funeral.

'The kingdom of heaven is like merchants seeking fine pearls and when they found the pearl of great price, they sold everything that they had, to have that pearl.'

The Parable of the Pearl – Matthew 13: 45-46

Geraldine's Pearl by Marcia M

Whoosh! I received an immense insight as it was then that I 'got' grandma's vocalisations of this verse when I was in troubled times. I accepted that she was not only telling me that I was special but that I was super special and of the highest value. WOW! My eyes and heart had opened up! "You are a pearl of great price Marcia." I mused over the words and realised that I was worthy of better and of more in every which way, from this place, my love of self began to grow.

Chapter Twenty-Eight

Closure

At the opening of this book I shared with you one of the experiences that affected me for many years, the memory of sexual abuse. The memory itself was very disturbing but what had haunted me throughout my life, was the fact that it had not been confirmed or acknowledged. You see when the crime took place there was a witness to it, an adult male in my family, who actually put a stop to the already heinous act progressing any further. He had scolded the perpetrator with "What are you doing? You should know better!" I had been saved somewhat from that terrible act against me going any further. I was five years of age. I only really acknowledged what had happened when I was in my teens. I had disclosed the incident to my mother when I was twenty-seven and my mother instantly believed me and was enraged and in her rage she had attempted to confront the perpetrator, but to no avail. My Journal entry read:

Geraldine's Pearl by Marcia M

"I was at a very low place in my life, trying to recover from the turmoil of my husband Vince's mental illness, so everything was a blur. Mom asked the older male if he recalled the incident, he said that he did not remember. So there I was, left with this haunting story in my mind, yet it had been denied."

It wasn't handled very well and I felt embarrassed and exposed, guilty almost. I chose to push it to the back of my mind and move on but then at the age of forty-three, I was sat with a friend who was now married to the male 'witness'. I had bravely confided in her about the memory, and she had been horrified and this had surprised me. The wonderful thing was, she acted upon the information I had shared with her. I hadn't asked her to but she spoke with her husband about it and telephoned me a few days later. I had never expected her to say anything to him; I had just been sharing my truth about my life.

Geraldine's Pearl by Marcia M

She told me "I asked him about what happened and he said he remembers and he remembers in detail!" My mouth fell open and a wave of relief engulfed me. This awful memory that had plagued me for thirty-seven years was now confirmed to be true and had not been my mind playing tricks on me. I shook and cried with relief as release and restoration were ignited within me.

"Oh my gosh" I said "Thank you. He remembered? Oh my gosh!" My breathing was erratic and I was overwhelmed and overjoyed and I wept thirty-eight years of suppressed tears over my anguish and my redemption.

I was content with the fact that the sexual assault had been confirmed and I felt that I had my closure. I did not want to take action or to prosecute, for me, closure had meant acknowledgement. So it was now and forever out of the way, as far as I was concerned.

However, the implementation of the confrontation process was taken out of my hands as I was the told that the perpetrator had himself been confronted by the 'witness',

and after being informed that I had remembered what had happened, his response had been: "Why now? Why is she bringing this up now?" Why now? I wasn't just 'bringing it up now', I had lived a lifetime of it being prevalently embedded in my every thought, particularly in the way that it had crept into my mind whenever I saw a little girl with a teenager. It had affected the way I parented my children and it had definitely impacted on my sexual liberty within my personal relationships. Then I was afforded the final chance to put closure to this ongoing nightmare.

In confronting my attacker, I had sought restorative justice by having a conversation with the perpetrator himself. I told him that I had always remembered and explained the ways that it had affected me throughout my whole life.

Geraldine's Pearl by Marcia M

The perpetrator admitted and acknowledged that it had happened and said that he himself had been in a 'bad place' at that time and that in his mind, it hadn't been me, Marcia that he had committed that act upon. I think I understand what he was saying: that growing up he couldn't connect the woman I am with the little girl who was traumatised and riddled with worry over a recurring memory.

Well it was me; it was I who had suffered because of his warped mind, yes me, the loving, bubbly, effervescent Marcia, who is standing before you. I told him "I forgive you" and I moved on to restoration, finally getting my personal closure to a dark and terrible secret.

Geraldine's Pearl by Marcia M

Chapter Twenty-Nine

I didn't know what I had lost until I found it.

At the beginning of this story, I told you about my older brother, Lionel, who was only six months older than me and that we were born into homes next door to one another. Well Lionel was missing from my life for over forty years and we were finally reconciled in December 2012 when he was in his mid-forties.

I had remembered playing with him once when we were children, yet he has no recollection of this, so as far as he was concerned, this was our first meeting. We had been jointly cared for by my mother when we were babies, this, we both would not have remembered, but maybe those early days had already given us the bond that we needed.

Geraldine's Pearl by Marcia M

It was just after Christmas and my sister Amanda and I were relaxing at my house, basking in that rich food and alcohol haze, you know that Christmas feeling. Uncle Bobby had called me; this was unusual as we didn't really speak to one another often. I had answered the telephone call curiously. "Hello" I said. "Marcia, I've got your brother here." I had thought for a minute. "My brother? Is this for real?" I had wondered. Uncle Bobby said, "Lionel is here and he wants to meet you!" Wow, my brother, our brother, the brother that I had remembered, the brother that I had asked about and searched for on the internet, was now here. Amanda and I hugged and grinned at the thought of finally being reunited with him.

We made our way to meet him, filled with curiosity and excitement.

So now there I was, standing before my older brother, my older sibling, "Are you my brother for real?"

He looked different to the way I had expected. He was very tall and well-built and also very handsome. My mom had always described him to be handsome, very good looking, she had said.

We hugged, we embraced for the first time and we cried well Amanda and I did, and he had whispered: "You are going to make a grown man cry here." He spoke with a South London accent and it was amazing, finally we were reunited.

We all got together, gathering our siblings and met at Leona's house and Adam made his way over for the reunion.

It was awesome. For the very first time, I was shifted into my place as the second child, not the eldest of my paternal family, grandchildren, but the second oldest. I was pleased to step aside and let the big man, my brother, take up his rightful position.

Geraldine's Pearl by Marcia M

Lionel had been named after one of the first born babies to my Grandparents'. The twin that had sadly died, our grandparents had thereafter blessed him with the name as he was their first, their extra special grandbaby, the one that changed their status from parents to grandparents. The 'first' are very important. Lionel, to a great extent, was robbed of his birth-right due to the circumstances surrounding his early childhood when his parents decided to move him away from our family, because they thought it was best for him. I totally understand that we all have to make difficult and painful decisions at times, when attempting to act in the interests of ourselves and our offspring.

In our forties, Lionel and I really connected and confided in each other as we shared so much of our lives with each other. It was like we had saved it all up to share with our best friend, once found and re-connected and the bond had been instantaneous, with the rapport and sense of 'knowing each other' with a mutual understanding, which had proved to be

Geraldine's Pearl by Marcia M

beyond any relationship I had previously known. We shared new experiences together for the first time, for example, celebrating bringing in the New year, walking in the snow together with me hanging on to him to save myself from slipping. We went to the cinema and celebrated my birthday with his daughter, my niece, who so happened to share the same birthdate as me, which had to have been more than a coincidence. We indulged in conversations of what ifs and what might have been had we grown up together, if I had really had an older brother and if he had had a sister like me.

We discovered that we had mutual acquaintances and had frequented some of the same venues in our teens, maybe we were even in the same places at the same time, but we would never have known.

For me, my sibling relationship with Lionel, is pivotal,

Geraldine's Pearl by Marcia M

It has helped to make my life complete. I have in him a friend, a brother and a confidante, that older person in whom I can trust implicitly. I am overjoyed at the depth of understanding, compassion and beauty of my brother's spirit. We also agreed that we are really brother and sister as our outlook on life is very similar although we have walked completely different paths.

My brother came into my life at a time when my actual career, in terms of employment, was breaking down and I was on the edge of a nervous breakdown. This was when I needed someone to be there for me, to support me. My elders were removed, grandma was not here, mom was abroad and grieving for the loss of her mother, my aunts and uncles too were struggling with the loss of grandma.

I had always felt responsible for the welfare and care of my younger siblings so did not want to burden them too much with my woes and problems.

Geraldine's Pearl by Marcia M

Lionel took his role as 'big brother' naturally and seriously and he told me, "Move over Sis, the real boss is here." He had a smile on his face but he meant it. I would retort gently, "You might be the older brother but I will always be the big sister and I am here for you." We had an understanding; we didn't really have to vie for position as I was honoured to accept all this love, care and firm advice from my 'older brother'. Just saying these words makes me feel safe and warm and loved and protected. I was overjoyed and felt like a little girl. I had an older brother that I needed and whom I had probably needed all of my life, through all of the scrapes and chaos.

Well now he was here and it was simply beautiful and what a beautiful person he was as was evident as we started to piece our stories together. We shared our life experiences and we truly connected, in fact, for me, it was like he had never been away, the feeling was so natural, it was as though throughout my whole life something had been missing and now I had found it!

Chapter Thirty

The Quest for Freedom

I had by then already embarked on my journey for healing and for peace and self-love, inclusive of being fortunate enough to gain access to life and performance coaching for myself. Within these sessions, I discovered that I was a teacher and a coach. I visualised the life that I wanted to create for myself, a life where I was able to be creative, in which I would spend quality time with my children, (I was not a grandmother then), and a life in which I would be an author, speaker and have a high profile coaching practice. It was also a vision that specified how the key word throughout it all would be FREEDOM!

In my coaching sessions, I cried bucket loads of tears as so many hidden heartaches surfaced and I wept some more in realising the revelation of my feelings about it all.

Geraldine's Pearl by Marcia M

Over time, I was able to slowly and progressively heal. The act of sharing in a safe space with someone whom I trusted implicitly and with whom I had felt safe, loved and respected, had kick-started my healing.

The major obstacle for me was my feelings about my various relationships with the people that I worked with, my boss, my deputy and my staff team. For most of my time in my role as a Senior Manager in Sure Start Children's Centres, I had suffered with stress, largely brought about by the various personal circumstances that I had endured and the periods during which I had been very depressed and extremely anxious.

I truly loved and respected my Boss as he was someone whom I had known for some time before I took up the position. When I started he commended me for my leadership ability affirming, "Marcia, you have a way of bringing people along" or "Well done, you handled that situation very well."

Geraldine's Pearl by Marcia M

I hit the ground running, it was my dream role. Whilst I had managed every type of child care service and run training centres, community enterprises and was qualified in social work, this job was a big one that would encompass all of the above disciplines and more. I achieved some major successes in the role and set up effective systems and structures. My staff also responded really well and gave me feedback about my fairness and interaction with them. I also loved and cared about my Deputy and I felt a great appreciation and affinity towards her. I had to work with her to develop her management and leadership skills and I supported her whole-heartedly, and she in turn, along with my Manager, provided me with support when my family and marriage difficulties had overwhelmed me. They had listened and they had rallied around to ensure that the service was delivered despite my need to take time off on quite a regular basis.

I realised that my being away from my role had left my team anchorless.

Geraldine's Pearl by Marcia M

I also believe that with my absence they had lost a great deal of confidence in me as their Leader, thus an informal team hierarchy ensued as they had to get through in my absence. I had no choice but to take those absences such was the gravity of my personal situation. From this unfortunate position, the mistrust had developed.

I had moved from a Chief Officer position for an African Caribbean Organisation that served a multi-ethnic community, to a full White staff team and a 95% White Community: these facts did not phase me when applying and taking up the position, however, the cultural, moral and sociological and intellectual gulf between me and my team was vast.

I was a Black woman in my mid-thirties, a Senior Manager, a career woman, a single parent divorcee and a practicing Christian and although I was younger than most of my team, I had the oldest child of the group and also the youngest.

Geraldine's Pearl by Marcia M

I also earned significantly more than they did. These factors set me apart and that was OK. I was used to being a Manager and Leader, I am different and that is really fine and accepted by me. I did find myself struggling as almost all of the women were married and they were the second income earners in their households, they spoke of their social activities and their annual holidays and I just could not relate. I was still battling with my teenage children's dilemmas, worrying times that I could not share because they would be horrified: you know how you couldn't just say, "My son is in a gang" or "By the way, my son could have been murdered" or "My daughter's been missing all weekend again." I just couldn't share this, not with the team anyway. I did confide in my Deputy a lot, in fact, in hindsight, it was too much, it was too much for her to handle, especially when she needed me to guide her in her work.

Despite my suffering I was still a Leader who would recognise good work and give recognition for it.

Geraldine's Pearl by Marcia M

I would be very honest with my feedback about areas where performance and professionalism needed to be improved. I had to educate them about basics like their references to Black people as 'coloured' and about the way that they handled people whose first language was not English. It was rare to have a Black family use the centre. I think it took about two years before I saw a Black person accessing the services.

I lived alone with my children and then went to work and was, in the main, alone. The reception of me was quite comical at times especially when I went out into the community in the village area at the edge of Sandwell. Despite me being the Head of the Services, there was an air of supremacy from the White staff and individuals in the community: "Ah, so you are the new helper?" They would ask. I would smile and look at one of my staff, for them to introduce me correctly; they would hesitate and almost stutter over the words: "No, she is the Programme Manager", flushing as they said it.

Geraldine's Pearl by Marcia M

I used to chuckle about those moments when I got home in the evenings. I also looked very young; I was in my mid-thirties but looked about twenty-seven or so. This didn't really faze me as I was by then, a very experienced leader and strategic and operational manager. I had achieved successes in many roles, turning newly developed and or failing organisations around. I had run my own business and many community-led businesses and I had all of the required credentials.

I discovered that there was a lack of loyalty and honesty and I was hypersensitive to their actions and took everything very personally.

An extract from my Journal:

'At my worst, my low mood and anxiety would render me stiff with fear of entering my place of work and at times I froze at the front entrance and struggled to control the feelings of nausea that gripped me as I sat in my car.

Geraldine's Pearl by Marcia M

I don't want to go, but I had to. I had taken my time to dress myself in what I realised was my armour. Perfectly straightened long hair extensions, precisely manicured nails including some rhinestones for a touch of bling, a smart pinafore dress, blouse and jacket, tights and heels with coordinating handbag, iPad case, mobile telephone case, pen and diary with matching earrings and not to mention matching underwear.

Perfectly applied make-up, sometimes with false lashes. It would take me hours to dress for the day, leaving me with piles of clothes and shoes all over the floor of my bedroom and bed and there they would remain until I returned home from work.

Anyway, now I was ready to face the day, I couldn't allow anyone outside to see my pain, my weakness and my needs.

Geraldine's Pearl by Marcia M

I was ready to face the world. I remember standing at the door of my Team's Office, feeling weak and afraid to enter, fear of real or perceived attacks, with constant thoughts running through my head of how I know they hate me, I know they are talking about me, how can I hold myself together and make it through the day.

I felt so lonely, so isolated, so judged and unloved. I was the Senior Manager and I felt powerless, victimised, bullied.

I would walk to my office gracefully and close the door and the blinds and cry. On occasions the staff saw me cry then would talk about it with one another and laugh at me. I was aware of this and felt even worse. I remember I used to stand in the doorway of my Line Manager and his team and feel that I did not exist; I had no relevance, no value. My confidence, my self-esteem, my quality of life had gone downhill. It seemed that they did not even notice that I was standing there.

Geraldine's Pearl by Marcia M

I cried a great deal at work. I cried on a daily basis to my Deputy about my daughter's illness, my abusive marriage, my grief at the loss of my grandparents. I lived alone and I was in so much pain but I did not speak about it. I isolated myself; it seemed that no-one would care. I was never asked if I was OK, I just wasn't. I stopped going to family functions, my hair fell out, I became stiff with arthritis, and I gained three stones. I felt as if I was dying. I went to work and church and still no-one asked and I wasn't going to say.

I just kept up this façade of showing the best of me on the outside because what would they think of me at church? They had already said that I should have submitted to my husband and when I cried in church they suggested I was not holy enough, not Godly enough but I was in pain and needed to heal. When I arrived at work stiff-faced and hardly speaking, they assumed that I was just being a 'bitch'. But I pushed myself not to show a crack in my armour so I dressed up and I glamorised and I pretended whilst inside every day I was in a void, I was crying. I was dying.'

Geraldine's Pearl by Marcia M

I needed to raise the funds to pay for my training as a Coach. I didn't have any savings so I wrote a list of what I needed including the money of £3,500. I also stated "Do not let the job get in the way, it is a means to an end" and I stuck the list on my fridge and at the top of the list in large letters, was the word 'FREEDOM'. I would glance at the list daily. This was my 'vision board'. I had written down my vison and made it clear to the Universe and then did hardly anything about it. The money for the training came and I got qualified as a coach, a trainer and a teacher.

I was able to cope with work as my sights were set on my Freedom, I had come to the realisation that I had been caring for my staff, my clients and the organisations that I worked for more that I cared for myself. So eventually took five months off sick, on full pay, during which time I took time out to grieve and recover. I spent time alone at home, resting, sleeping, and also spending some quality time with friends and family.

I took time to reflect on who I was and on who I wanted to be. My surname had changed so many times from being married, separated and divorced twice and I had a choice between choosing any of my former surnames but chose to officially change back to my original birth name.

After a little while, I embarked on further personal developmental training and I also ran my Coaching and Events business which was at that time a serious hobby during which time I invested my funds and resources into developing other people alongside myself. I didn't really need to generate income from it as my earnings were now nearing £50k per annum. At the end of the five-months sick period, I took redundancy from my job and was finally FREE from a chain that had held me for eight years, a chain that I had desired to break free from but just had not had the courage to do so.

Geraldine's Pearl by Marcia M

Leaving my job was a major expression of self-love. I was a workaholic, my focus had always been on achieving and being approved of and following my mantra of 'the greatest revenge is success'. However, I was mistaken; I hadn't understood that the greatest success and achievement was not external validation but a love and appreciation of my own self.

In my neurolinguistics programming training it was soon unveiled to me that I held a limiting belief that I was not good enough, despite my relative career successes. I held self-loathing and devaluing thoughts about myself subconsciously.

Geraldine's Pearl by Marcia M

I didn't feel that I deserved better. I had consciously thought that I loved me but I realised that I was holding onto the thoughts that I was a failure, that I was not deserving of a better quality of life and relationships. I attracted people who loved the exterior of me, my face, and they objectified me so much so that they could not love me because all they could see was this projected fantasy of the real me. I also hadn't fully recovered from my self-doubt and body dysmorphia, particularly in terms of my nose, my shape, weight and ankles.

This may sound ridiculous but negative comments made about these parts of my body had penetrated my spirit and I had allowed my perception of self to be broken. I didn't really know who I was and I had been too busy running on the treadmill of life and had never pressed the stop button. I was used to fighting fires of chaos and dealing with catastrophes and creating what I viewed as success, a good, solid career through promotions and study.

Geraldine's Pearl by Marcia M

I had lived with decades of anxiety, worrying, planning, avoidances and I had stubbornly held on to phobias, I didn't like being looked at, I felt awkward and inadequate, I didn't take photographs or even dance because of my insecurity and low self-esteem. I would rather not wear anything too vibrant or sexy for fear of seeming too much. I preferred to blend into the background and watch friends and loved ones enjoying life in the lime-light.

I was next introduced to 'The Three Principles'. My Coach and I met for lunch and she pulled out a glittery bouncing ball and said "Marcia, look at this ball, the glitter flakes moving around represent your thoughts." As she shook the ball my stomach churned, it was true, every shake of the ball and the glitter just moved about erratically and randomly like my thoughts. I was gripped by the concept that she explained to me but I didn't quite get it. I asked her for the ball as it fascinated me. She explained that when I allowed my thoughts to settle I would get clarity and could access innate wisdom for my life. I understood the principles to be a fundamental ancient paradigm, a way of looking at life, a way of living and being.

Geraldine's Pearl by Marcia M

My quest for more knowledge of 'The Three P's' began then and I read the books that were recommended and watched the videos. Learning about 'The Three Principles' allowed me to slow down my very busy and anxious mind. I learnt that I didn't have to try to control my life circumstances but could actually let go.

When I got the understanding, my overthinking reduced. I would still at times, go back to my old ways, but I was able to correct myself much more quickly and the more that I let go and aligned myself with nature, it had a way of correcting situations itself. I learnt to be still and be quiet, to truly listen and hear particularly, the unspoken internal communication. Life began to flow more naturally at a pace that was not forced. I understood and accepted that I was not in control of my life, I never was and I never will be.

Geraldine's Pearl by Marcia M

I understood that I am a beautiful person, deserving of love and that the first place for that love to exude from, was me. I now know it's true that my life experiences start from my own thinking and that I have the choice to decide on how and what I think, I cannot control my thoughts but I can choose whether to believe them. You see, thoughts come and go, they are like bubbles which when blown up, can be seen and they exist in that moment but the bubbles soon disappear, this is what thought is, they appear just as real as the first ones but still different, this is like fresh thought, thoughts come and thoughts go. We do not have to hold onto old or toxic thoughts at all, we can let them go.

Geraldine's Pearl by Marcia M

I attended a 'Three Principles' conference in June 2012 and sat and listened to a well-respected mentor in the community. I was in a room filled with men and women of all races and faiths. We listened intently to the stories told by our speaker. There were times when I was so relaxed that I drifted off to sleep, however, miraculously, every time I woke up, I was up to speed with the presentation, which was strange. I hadn't missed anything that I was supposed to hear.

Our Mentor told us about a young boy who explained that he would 'fall out of himself' to get to a place of consciousness. In that instant I felt a flow of love engulf me that was so very powerful it was awesome.

Geraldine's Pearl by Marcia M

I had felt that feeling many years before when I was in church. I had explained this to my Mentor who gently stated, "Yes Marcia, we touch the very essence of the true and living God" – that for me was an almighty experience, the real life-changer. I then began to see things that I had never seen before, trees, buildings and people, I noticed interactions and heard and saw like never before. I became aware of seeing beyond the surface, beyond the words and reached inside of myself for healing. I came to know that everything I needed, every answer for my life, was within me, my innate wisdom and ultimate well-being. I came to know that life is a beautiful gift to all human kind and that I am a beautiful gift to the world. I was enabled to see beauty in others that I had never seen and have tolerance and patience for them.

Please do not misunderstand me, I am not now perfect, I still have doubts and worries but now I know how to recover much more quickly.

Geraldine's Pearl by Marcia M

I spend a lot of time doing nothing and just allowing my life to unfold before me. Every desire of my heart is being manifested and I believe that this is because I have tuned out of my head-thinking and zoned in into innate wisdom, that knowledge that comes from a deep connection with the Divine and Universal higher powers.

You see, everything that we experience, whether it is of form, meaning an object that we can see, taste or touch, or formless within our minds, is created by thoughts. Our actions and reactions come from what we are thinking in the moment. Living moment by moment and choosing not to see the positive or negative of a situation but rather stay in 'neutral' enables me to achieve peace and wellness.

I was told once to 'touch everything lightly' and I understood this to mean don't take things so seriously or personally, just pass it by like the touch of a feather, let worries and upsets just flow in and out or wash over me.

Geraldine's Pearl by Marcia M

The most powerful learning from this insight for me was to live in the present, the here and the right now, to choose not to dwell on the past or to concern myself with the future. This has enabled the enjoyment of every little thing, tastes, touch, sounds and vibrations. Routines, regimes, rules and rigidity no longer being necessary, these are replaced with organic flow, spontaneity and adventure.

I really truly love me and I also love others, the more that I have found love for me has enhanced my capacity to love and be compassionate. The episodes in the previous chapters of this book are past and distant memories, enabling me to gain wisdom and knowledge in the present moment. My relationships with my children are closer and deeply connected.

Geraldine's Pearl by Marcia M

Chapter Thirty-One

'Suicide Disease'

I am diagnosed with a chronic neurological/nervous system illness known commonly as 'the suicide disease'. 'Trigeminal neuralgia' (TN), is considered to be one of the most painful afflictions known in medical practice. Trigeminal Neuralgia is a disorder of the fifth cranial (trigeminal) nerve. The typical or 'classic' form of the disorder causes extreme sporadic, sudden burning or shock-like facial pains in the areas of the face where the branches of the nerve are distributed – lips, eyes, nose, scalp, forehead, upper jaw, and lower jaw. The intense flashes of pain can be triggered by vibration or contact with the cheek, brushing your teeth, eating, drinking, talking or being exposed to the wind. People with TN avoid social contact and daily activities such as eating and talking because they fear a repeat onset of the disease in public.

Geraldine's Pearl by Marcia M

Many have been known to lose their jobs because of the debilitating nature of the pain. Marriages have dissolved due to the difficulty of providing care and support to persons with TN. Pain from TN is frequently very isolating and depressing for the individual. Depression and sleep disturbance may render individuals vulnerable to pain and suffering. All of this ultimately results in a high cost of suffering from this disease, in regards to individuals, families and social aspects. There is an extremely high incidence of sufferers taking their own lives as they feel it is the only way to end the pain.

In September 2014 I endured thirty days of this severe pain except for one day when I had a stroke experience, whereby my left side froze. I was very unwell and my children tell me that when they saw me in that pain, lying in bed unable to speak or eat or be touched, they were terrified that I was going to die. My youngest daughter had to grow up fast. Gerry had to take on the full responsibilities of cooking meals, washing clothes and getting herself to and from school.

Geraldine's Pearl by Marcia M

Her father Eric and my son Solomon were in Jamaica at the time and it was upsetting for them to hear that I was so ill and that they were so many miles away. The years that had passed since Gerry was born had brought me and Eric so close that we now lived like brother and sister. Eric, whilst all the way in Jamaica, must have arranged with his sister in England, for her and his niece to come around and take care of me and Gerry, with the pregnancy animosity long forgiven and forgotten.

When you are suffering with a pain that is described as 'the most severe pain known to medicine', you cannot focus on anything but the pain, in fact nothing else exists but pain.

My parents would call me on 'face-time' every morning and ask how I was feeling. All I could do was to lie there and whisper, "Pain. Pain." I couldn't say much else, despite their expressions of compassion and concern.

Geraldine's Pearl by Marcia M

I would hold the side of my face to protect it, the pain just made my face feel so sensitive to touch and looking so shrunken. To drink something hot or cold I would have to use a straw and would have to eat mashed and soft foods and chewing would bring on more pain. The pain would shoot through my ear, my eye, the tip of my nose, my cheeks, in my gums, my teeth and literally almost every surface part of my face. Regular pain relief tablets would not touch the pain, I could not sleep because of pain, and I could not do anything. At the time of the stroke experience where my left side completely froze, I was taking a cocktail of approximately seventy tablets a week which was then increased to approximately one hundred and fifty-four tablets including medications for anti-epilepsy, anti-convulsion, anti-depressants and nerve pain control.

I was dependant on medication for about six months at this acute level. The main side-effects were drowsiness, and then an additional complication happened when one morning I woke up and tried to lift my head. As I did so, the room spun around and around like a tornado. It was so scary that I couldn't get up.

"Oh my God! I'm having a stroke" I thought. I couldn't move. I struggled to get up but then had to give in and lie down flat again. It was terrifying and for about ten long minutes I had to just lie down and be still. As the feeling started to pass, I heard myself gasp: "What's happening to me?" My son came and took me to an emergency doctor who diagnosed vertigo and I was prescribed even more medication to prevent the nausea and vomiting that is commonly associated with vertigo. I fell over a number of times when getting dressed because my balance had gone.

Geraldine's Pearl by Marcia M

Even through this illness, my default for survival, my desire to achieve, my drive and my ambition were not halted. I must admit that there were days that in the haze of all of that medication I still drove the car to the local college were I taught nursing classes for three full days. I was heavily medicated, drowsy and with a dry and droopy mouth. I don't know how I did it and I don't know why, but I did.

I also attended 'Mastermind' sessions for my business development. I was very unwell but again, through the pain and meds, I risked an accident to drive to these meetings. Crazy and ridiculous you may think and I agree, but such was my determination to overcome and beat this disease.

Geraldine's Pearl by Marcia M

My behaviour was as though I was superhuman; it was crazy. I should have been in bed. Even with the vertigo, I would call a taxi in order to get to work and tried to control the dizziness whilst teaching. I had to suck sweets throughout the lessons and sip water to manage the dryness in my mouth. Sometimes I could not hear or see properly in the classes but I fought my way through. I had to keep going, a voice inside me encouraged and willed me to be well.

The illness took me completely off my feet for three months; my whole body was fighting against the pain. The pain started to ease when the dosage of medications finally worked and it was then discovered that the whole of my left side was in agony. My arm, leg, torso and shoulders required massage treatments and I had salt baths to wash my limbs but they really hurt during all of this.

Geraldine's Pearl by Marcia M

The left side of my body had been through a massive trauma, manifesting in this pain that has no cure. After the stroke scare, I had slept solid for seven days and seven nights, remaining cocooned in bed, only getting up to go to the bathroom or to take my medications. Other than that, I slept constantly, as if heavily sedated. Some of my family and friends really rallied around for me all during this horrible time: cooking meals, tidying up, looking out for Gerry and some people really surprised me with their kindness.

I couldn't really entertain visitors as I was too ill. It was frustrating for my mother as she was unwell at the same time too so couldn't come to my aid. My sister Amanda became my main caregiver, she represented mom, she has a tender loving way of caring for me that is extra special. My brother Lionel was also very supportive and he cooked me meals and kept me company along with my cousin Liz.

Geraldine's Pearl by Marcia M

Even Eric, on his return from Jamaica, came straight from the airport to see me and a couple of my old school and college friends also visited all showing kindness and love. Lionel, Liz and I giggled at some strange habits that I had developed in that time, for example, I used to keep repeating myself over and over and I started to swear! Swear words flew out of my mouth randomly like tics, my desire to smoke also returned, all were weird things but then we were dealing with a huge malfunction related to the brain plus masses of pharmaceuticals, so no wonder some of my behaviours were bizarre.

This all happened in the midst of re-branding and re-launching my business. I was wounded physically, socially and financially. I was unable to cope with going out to places, I needed to take plenty of rest. I could not hug or have close physical contact with anyone. When I laid down my head would spin.

Geraldine's Pearl by Marcia M

I used to think *'God forbid if I tried to have sex, I wouldn't cope as my head would be in a spin and I would probably vomit'. It was mostly just a thought but it was also a slight fear, would I be able to live a normal life again? Am I now disabled? Can I actually work? How will I make my living?*

Being in that type of pain taught me how to be still and how to completely surrender. Being in that stillness, I was no longer in control. I was not in control of the pain and I was not in control of my healing. The only thing that I could do was just be still and to allow nature to take its course to provide the healing. That illness taught me to appreciate the simple things in life.

The illness was a gift and it was an opportunity to gain more wisdom and understanding. The day that I opened my eyes and there was no pain was the most wonderful experience of my life, to actually wake up and there was no pain.

Geraldine's Pearl by Marcia M

I learnt to appreciate the simplest gift of just being alive and being free, no more pain. Also in that cocoon, curled up in my bed, I learnt about what was important, I learnt about love and care, I learnt about family and I could see my life completely differently. The way that I thought about things became so simplified, the priorities for life, the freedom just to be able to begin to live again was just a marvellous, empowering, freeing and loving moment.

I returned to a place where I had to re-build, but I had all of the resources I needed. I decided that I was not ill. I decided that I was well. I decided that I was not disabled. A month later the illness went into remission. Apart from that episode twelve months ago, on occasions I have had short bouts of taking meds and resting, maybe four times in one year. I am really well and everything is good.

Geraldine's Pearl by Marcia M

Epilogue

I am Marcia M

"For God has not given us a spirit of fear, but of power and of love and of a sound mind" 2 Timothy 1:7 (NKJV)

I AM Marcia M.

My name is Marcia I am fearless and I am free. I am free to live, to love and to be, to simply be myself, my true self. I am attracting everything that I need by letting go, by surrendering and by no longer trying to do the working out. I don't have to work it out as my life was not created by me, I am not the author or the finisher; I am a human, just being me.

I am blessed to have been given the life that I have lived and the wealth and richness of experiences. I am thankful for all of the lessons learnt and for lessons to come.

Geraldine's Pearl by Marcia M

Pain is no longer my enemy. I learnt through pain, be it physical or psychological pain, that it is OK to be still and that all will be well. In fact, everything is Okay. I do not stress over finances either as all of my provisions are supplied.

The wheel of my life is being turned by a force beyond me so therefore I am free to enjoy the simple things, the moments like right now, lying on my bed on a February Sunday morning. It's actually Valentine's Day 2016. I am a single, twice married divorcee and despite having a number of suitors and admirers, I have not yet attracted the partner who can truly compliment me and yet still I am feeling truly loved, complete and at peace.

Marcia M.

Geraldine's Pearl by Marcia M

Geraldine's Pearl is an introduction to my story, I will continue to share in books two and three of this Trilogy. My second book will be about sharing the nuances of being single, married, separated and divorced twice, a book about love, sex and romance.

@copyrights 2016 Marcia M.

Would you like to find out more about how I was able to heal and move on from my memories?

Contact me www.marciamspence.com

Email: Confidence@marciamspence.com

About the Author:

Marcia M is an award winning woman as An extraordinary woman who has touched lives- she is winner of a Star Award 2015 and the coveted Star of ALL Stars 2015

Nominations for: BEFFTA Radio Personality 2015: The Phoenix: Business Award Finalist 2015

- A Time to Change Champion, working to end mental health Stigma and Discrimination.
- An Ambassador for FREE YOUR MIND CIC Raising awareness of the Impact of Domestic Abuse on Children.
- A member and ambassador for the Trigeminal Neuralgia Association UK.
- A friend of OSCAR Sandwell support and research for sickle cell disease.

Marcia M.
Marcia is a woman who has chosen to share her vast knowledge, skills and experience with other women across the globe. Branded as 'The Success Maker' and the CEO of Success Makers and Marcia M Spence, she is a personal and professional development facilitator. Marcia says "My mission is to provide support, encouragement, training and mentoring to women who are professionals, leaders, aspirational women who experience the diverse pressures of balancing the responsibilities of home, family, work and self."

Geraldine's Pearl by Marcia M

Marcia is also quoted as saying: "I have had reason to have to find strength and a multitude of instinctive survival strategies to overcome personal circumstances including divorce, single parenthood, chronic illness, lack of confidence and self-esteem. I believe that I have perfected 'Bounce-back-ability' - the ability to bounce back, to keep on driving forward, not to accept the knock-backs but to learn from them and use them as stepping stones and this has become my art. My greatest achievement has been to finally and truly love myself and because of this, I refuse to accept less than I am worth. I was born a leader and I honestly believe that leaders are born. However, I also have the hope that leadership skills can be developed in any one who is determined enough."

Marcia M is a dynamic manager and developer of groups and individuals and has led teams since the age of twenty. She specialises in identifying potential, growing leaders and releasing power and repairing self-esteem. Marcia shares her extensive experiences with others at all levels, utilising her range of communication and facilitation skills, including Coaching, Training, Mentoring and Motivational and Inspirational speaking. Marcia has almost thirty years' experience in the creation, establishment and delivery of services for children, women and their families within the public and community sectors and as a self-employed childcare and training provider across the West Midlands.

Geraldine's Pearl by Marcia M

As a community activist, Marcia has succeeded in Campaigning for quality services and equality issues as well as Researching and implementing Community Regeneration projects and Social Enterprise. Marcia's interest in coaching evolved naturally over two decades when many people turned to her for support and encouragement, both for their career development and for personal issues and these efforts earned her the title 'Success Maker'. Marcia also had the benefit of accessing Life and Performance Coaching for herself for a period of three years and this experience transformed her life.

Marcia says, "I have no doubt that what we think about can become our reality, and that we have the power to create our own reality through our thoughts. Since embracing 'The Three Principles of Mind, Thought and Consciousness', my life is of the highest quality ever, as I am able to live my life effortlessly, with love and understanding".

Marcia M

Marcia M has devised and hosts the now Iconic Radio Talk Show "On the Couch with Marcia M Spence".

On the Couch™ is a Radio talk show in a relaxed atmosphere like a family and friends getting together on a Sunday afternoon. We have real conversations about real issues that affect their day to day lives and their loved ones. Taboo subjects that families often don't discuss in an open forum are explored on

Geraldine's Pearl by Marcia M

the show, in a safe environment where guest are honoured and respected for their personal journeys.

There are usually at least three people involved in the conversation but often many more and we take calls from the listening audience too.

On the Couch™ Live is the Talk Show with a live audience, speakers, special guest and entertainment this is not aired on radio but provides a platform to explore issues deeper and for the promotion of talent, Businesses and Entrepreneurs, Authors and other Creatives & Artistes. This has been featured at The Birmingham Repertory Theatre, The Park Inn Hotels and is now also an inspirational column in a woman's Magazine.

On the Couch™ is an excellent platform to launch yourself and connect with your audience.

Coming soon On the Couch™ TV talk show!

On the Couch™ is a trademark of Marcia M Spence, The Success Maker. Podcasts are available on MixCloud.

Marcia is has recently been dubbed "Interviewer Extraordinaire" after the interviews that she conducted On the Couch at The Birmingham Repertory Theatre.

Woman of Power and Influence #WPI is another of Marcia M. Spence Trademarks

A personal and professional development programme The Programme is aimed at women who are aiming to move to the top of their field to expand their current projects and business. For women who are aspiring to move in to leadership roles and who are ready to become more dynamic as a professional. If you are facing a major change of direction in your career then this Programme is for you!

©marciamspence.com2016

Testimonials about the Author

"Those who genuinely know what it takes to operate at a senior level also know what a lonely place management can be. It is imperative you surround yourself with people like yourself or people you desire to emulate. For me, that person is Marcia M Spence, who is not only a friend, confidante and inspiration, but she is someone I can talk seriously with about politics, systems and processes, making decisive decisions, life, culture, recreation or silly, funny things simply for our amusement. There are not many people with whom you can socialise and work professionally with, I was able to do both because Marcia M Spence was a phenomenal woman of knowledge, experience and insight."

Aeon Anderson - Manager St Basils

Geraldine's Pearl by Marcia M

"Wow, what can I say, where do I start? Anyway, here goes! I have known Marcia now for nearly 4 years and all I can say is, 'truly inspirational.' I feel like we've been on a journey, a journey that throughout, all I've seen is a woman who has been determined, focused, supportive and fun, words alone can't explain. I'm so proud to have this woman of influence as my mentor and friend. You have been all the above and more but most of all in my opinion you have been truly and definitely 'The Success Maker'. I love you Marcia M and I look forward to the future with you. I'm so proud of you for doing what you know has to be done. It wasn't easy but you've done it anyway. Thank You for being an example. Much Love"
Yanique Taylor – Beauty Specialist

Marcia you have an amazing ability to create safe spaces for people to heal and grow, Your personal journey is phenomenal: you are a truly strong, authentic and natural leader. Thank you for investing in my life – **Tina Allen Mixed Harmony Group – Geraldine's Pearl Award Winner 2015**

@copyright Marcia M 2016

Geraldine's Pearl by Marcia M

Made in the USA
Charleston, SC
25 June 2016